W0050160

MAKE
EPIC
MONEY

MAKE EPIC MONEY

ANKUR WARIKOO

PENGUIN
BUSINESS

An imprint of Penguin Random House

PENGUIN BUSINESS

Penguin Business is an imprint of the Penguin Random House group of companies
whose addresses can be found at global.penguinrandomhouse.com

Published by Penguin Random House India Pvt. Ltd
4th Floor, Capital Tower 1, MG Road,
Gurugram 122 002, Haryana, India

Penguin
Random House
India

First published in Penguin Business by Penguin Random House India 2024

Copyright © Ankur Warikoo 2024

All rights reserved

10 9 8 7 6 5 4 3

This book is a work of non-fiction. The views and opinions expressed in it are those
of the author only and do not reflect or represent the views and opinions held by any
other person. This book is based on a variety of sources, including published materials,
research conducted by the author and personal experiences of the author. It reflects the
author's own understanding and conception of such materials and events. The author
is not a registered investment, legal or tax adviser, or a broker/dealer. All opinions
expressed in the book are from the personal research and experience of the author
and are not intended and should not be understood or construed as financial advise.
Readers are advised to do their own analysis and take independent professional advise
before making any investment or financial decisions. The objective of this book is
not to hurt any sentiments or be biased in favour of or against any particular person,
corporate entity, region, caste, society, gender, creed, territory, nation or religion.

ISBN 9780670099818

Typeset in League Spartan by Manipal Technologies Limited, Manipal
Printed at Thomson Press India Private Limited

This book is sold subject to the condition that it shall not, by way of trade or otherwise,
be lent, resold, hired out, or otherwise circulated without the publisher's prior consent
in any form of binding or cover other than that in which it is published and without a
similar condition including this condition being imposed on the subsequent purchaser.

www.penguin.co.in

Dedicated to the rupees I wasted and the wisdom I earned

CONTENTS

INTRODUCTION

Congratulations!

You've picked the least likely author of a book on money!
-   I'm not an expert.
-   I don't have the right degrees.
-   My money history? Pretty disastrous.

I'm not as cool as Ramit Sethi. Not as articulate as Morgan Housel.
Nowhere near as knowledgeable as Deepak Shenoy or Monika Halan.

So, if you're skimming this online or in a bookstore, this is your chance to escape, my friend.
Put this book away! 😬

But if you already have this book, imagine me in an Instagram reel, giving you:

3 reasons to read *Make Epic Money*:

1.   We learn more from those who have made mistakes than from those who haven't.
     I've made many. Learnt from each one. Picked myself up.
     I'd love for you to not make the same mistakes I made.

2.   I wonder why most books on money are so complex. Technical, intimidating, long.
     This book tries to answer one simple question:
     How can a book on money be both helpful and joyful for those in their 20s/30s, who've grown up in the Instagram and YouTube era?

3.   I'm not trying to impress (I don't even have the qualifications to do so).

I'm trying to help. To make finance fun.
This book will speak your language, not mine.
It will use your words, not mine.

Oh, before I move on.
Remember the golden rule: It's the book's job to hold your attention as much as it is yours to give it attention.
So if, at any point, this book becomes boring, drop it! No pressure.
There are more awesome books on money out there.
If you're still with me, here's the backstory.
Of money and me.

We grew up without money.

My dad worked in sales and marketing for almost all his career. Mom was a primary school teacher.

A family aspiring to escape the middle-class curse.

Credit cards. Personal Loans. Buying more than we could afford.

Those were the methods we used.

We were always in debt. Unsurprisingly.

My parents' dreams for financial security (maybe even prosperity!) were pinned on my sister and me.

I was told there was a proven process for achieving it:

- Study hard
- Get a good job
- Work hard
- Get promoted
- Earn well
- Live happily ever after

I was convinced.

So I studied hard. Became the teacher's pet.
Won a scholarship for a PhD in the US.
Pursued an MBA. Became a management consultant.
Earned well.
Then became a founder, with dreams of becoming a billionaire!

I spent my 20s and 30s chasing a plan that I was convinced would work for me. Until it didn't.
At 39, I had no money in the bank.
I had stepped down as the CEO of my start-up and had no source of income.
I had paper wealth that did not amount to anything.
No assets to speak of.
Plus a family to take care of.

FML! HOW could this have happened?

I reflected. Read. Listened. Thought. Deciphered.

And figured that no one—school, college, parents—had taught me anything about money.

All that I was taught was how to earn a living.

Frankly, this book is for the 20-year-old me.
And for everyone like me.
Who was prescribed a blueprint for life but was never told how to manage money.
Or how to make money work for me.

Make Epic Money has a simple message.

Your background. Insufficient knowledge. Limited experience. Lack of expertise.
These are NOT the things that hold you back from making money.
From building wealth.
From living the life you deserve.
What holds you back are your deep-rooted beliefs.

The beliefs that tell you that:
- Middle-class people rarely get rich.
- You have too many financial obligations.
- Money is too complicated to understand.
- Salary is the only source of income.
- Only rich or lucky people get wealthy.

Your beliefs can ruin you financially.
Or they can set you up for life.
Change your beliefs, change everything.

This book is an attempt to challenge and provoke you to change your beliefs.
So you don't make the same mistakes I made.

This book is designed to be a light read.
Each chapter is independent of the others.
So play around with it.

Every day, read a few pages.
Come back to it the next day.
When the book gets boring, drop it.

In the end, take 5 ideas from this book.
Your choice, any 5!
Apply them to your life. Follow them consistently.
Make them your unbreakable money beliefs.

If you do just this, you've started your journey to financial independence.
Towards building wealth.

I am excited for you! 😁

WHY SHOULD
I EVEN CARE
ABOUT MONEY?

'Money does not buy you happiness, but lack of money certainly buys you misery.'

—Daniel Kahneman

In Money We Trust. And That's Why It Works!

Let's figure out how money came into being in the first place.

We began with an exchange.

Picture this:
I want 1 egg.
You want 1 potato.
We agreed to exchange. Or barter, if you want to be fancy!

Simple enough.

But at some point, eggs become really valuable. Now to get 2 eggs, people want 7 potatoes in barter.

Okay, but what if I want only 1 egg?
That will exchange for 3.5 potatoes.
What's the deal with the fractions, bro?
No one else will trade for half a potato!

And what if I want 50 eggs?
I have to lug around 175 potatoes.
That's inconvenient.

Then, along came a wise dude.
'Give me your potatoes, and I'll hand you some pieces of paper.
Each paper is worth 1 potato or 0.5 or 2 potatoes or 5/10/20/50/100.'
'It's proof that I have your potatoes with me,' he said. *'Just bring the papers back if you ever want the potatoes.'*

And he puts a unique stamp on these papers to prove he's legit.
Now, instead of carrying the potatoes, I carry these pieces of stamped paper.
Genius!

That's pretty much how money started—at least the way we see it today.

Ever notice the statement 'I promise to pay the bearer the sum of five hundred rupees' on a ₹500 note, signed by the RBI governor?

That's our potato paper in its swanky new avatar!

Think about it for a second.

We trust a piece of paper, signed by someone whose name we most likely don't even know.

It's not just us—the entire world seems to trust this paper.

Irrespective of who they are or where they're from.

The supermarket gives you groceries in return for your paper notes because they trust the bank and the government to back the transaction.

You grind at work to get your salary credited to your bank account in the form of digital money you can't see.

But that's cool because Amazon, Flipkart, Paytm, Myntra, Google Pay, Mastercard, Visa—they all trust it, and they'll take it.
They may not know or trust you, but they trust money.

It's mind-blowing. Money only works because we all believe in it.
Money is the BEST example of trust in this world.

'Money is the only trust system created by humans that can bridge almost any cultural gap . . . It's the most universal and most efficient system of mutual trust ever devised.'

—Yuval Noah Harari, *Sapiens: A Brief History of Humankind*

Can Money Buy Happiness?

We use money every day, all the time.
We need it to survive.

But it's so much more than that!

While you might look at money as something with which to buy things and luxury, the TRUE power of money goes beyond that.

Here are 10 things that money can buy:

1. Peace of mind
    Knowing that school fees, EMIs, salaries are covered.
    Knowing that everyone you're responsible for is taken care of.

2. Health
    Quality health care. Insurance.
    Healthy food, gym memberships, fitness classes, wellness programmes.

3. Quality food
   Junk food is cheap for a reason. It's bad for us.
   Good-quality, healthy food is a luxury that money can buy.

4. Safety
   The privilege of having our own transport.
   Living in a safe neighbourhood. Being able to afford security.

5. Options
   This college or that?
   A job for learning or money?
   Take a break from work or continue the grind?
   Money lets us choose.

6. Comfort
   A quality mattress. Good shoes. Warm clothes.
   Heating, air conditioning, cool gadgets.

7. Courage

   Money backs us up when we take risks.
   Cushions the fear of failure.
   It helps us explore, learn and be audacious.

8. Happy family

   Money lets us surprise our parents, siblings,
   partners, friends with what they have
   always craved.

9. Experiences

   Travel, concerts, safaris, cruises, once-in-a-
   lifetime events.
   Experience the best of what the world has to
   offer.

10. Freedom

    To slow down, because we want to.
    Do more, because we want to.
    Live life how we want to.

The true purpose of money is NOT to help us buy things.

The true purpose of money is to grant us freedom—over our time, our choices and the way we lead our lives.

Imagine a world, where:
You wake up at your own pace, no alarm.
You have a lovely morning routine, doing things you love.
Have a nice, chill breakfast: you feel no rush.
You stay close to office. Or work from home. No traffic jams.
You work through the day. It's challenging work, but joyful work.
You genuinely enjoy your work.
In the evening you try something new, go for a swim, chill with friends or just relax.
You wind up the day, feeling grateful. No stress.

Total freedom to do
whatever you want,
whichever way you want,
whenever you want.

This is a life that we can build for ourselves. Once we understand how to stop working for money and, instead, make money work for us.

'The ability to do what you want, when you want, with who you want, for as long as you want to, pays the highest dividend that exists in finance.'

—Morgan Housel,
The Psychology of Money

NOW, I REALLY WANT TO EARN SOME MONEY!

'There's a limit to how much you can cut.
There's no limit to how much you can earn.'

—Ramit Sethi,
I Will Teach You to Be Rich

The world sells you a dream.
It tells you: Once you start earning a salary, you can become wealthy.

Here's the truth.
A salary helps you earn a living. But it also locks you in.
You trade your time for money.
If you stop giving your time, the money stops.
You'll have to work all your life.
Your salary is not enough.
If there is one belief you must change, let it be this one.

Wealthy people have it figured out.
They're wealthy because they don't build their lives around a salary.
They use their time and ideas to create multiple income streams.
They work for money. But they also put their money to work.

It's a different rule book.
One that we should all play by.

Financial Literacy: It Matters!

Since we are told that getting a job or starting a business is the only source of money, we chase degrees, impressive qualifications, fancy titles. Assuming that *professional success = rich*.

The truth?
Professional degrees help you earn a living.
Financial literacy helps you build wealth.

It's a life skill.

Without financial literacy, we risk making mistakes.
The most basic, avoidable mistakes.

1. No safety net
   Covid caught us off guard: expenses surged, hospital bills piled up, jobs were lost.
   Many of us had no insurance, no back-up— no safety net.
   When we needed them the most.

2. Spending more than we earn
   Impulsive buys, consumerism, EMIs.
   Draining our wallets, spending more than
   we earn.

3. Drowning in loans
   Hello, credit cards and loans with huge
   interest rates.
   We thought we could manage to pay them
   off. Now we're buried under a mountain
   of debt.

4. Playing it too safe
   Parking our money in savings accounts and
   fixed deposits.
   Just like our parents told us to.
   Guess what? Its value decreased every year.
   Inflation ate it up.

5. No future planning
   Turning a blind eye to financial goals.
   Spending money without knowing why.

Worse, not even knowing where our money is going every month.

6. Getting greedy
   Investing out of greed: easy gains, get-rich-quick schemes, 'tip-offs'.
   Makes us take the worst decisions.
   Investing out of fear: of missing out, of losses or market crashes, of being stuck with dead stocks.

This is what we do.
Aam aadmi, mango people.

The wealthy?
They play differently. They play smarter.

The secret is learning to think like a wealthy person.

Assets vs Liabilities: Spot the Difference, Accumulate Assets

Most of us don't really understand what an asset is.
And what a liability is.

Phones. Gadgets. Jewellery. Cars.
We call them assets because we own them.
Oh, and a house, the ultimate asset! Renting is so middle class.
So we keep buying things we think are assets.

Here is the only definition that matters:
Does it earn you money?
Yes? Then it's an asset.
No? Then it's simply a possession. Maybe even a liability.

'Rich people acquire assets. The poor and middle class acquire liabilities that they think are assets.'

—Robert T. Kiyosaki,
Rich Dad Poor Dad

Let's understand this with a few examples.

Car: Asset or liability?
You buy a car. As you drive out of the showroom it hits you that you don't really want it.
You just wanted to show off to your friends. Tell them you've arrived in life.

So you reverse into the showroom, apologize and ask, 'Could you please take this car back?'
The showroom owner hasn't heard this before, but he's a cool guy. Meets all kinds of people.
He says he'll take it back.
'I will pay you 90% of the price you paid me.'

Wait, WTF just happened?
Cars depreciate in value. Instantly! That's what happened.
And they keep depreciating, 10–20% every year.

Plus, loan interest, if you've taken a loan.
Maintenance, insurance, repairs.
Sorry, your car is a liability.

You have to keep spending money on it to own it.
That doesn't mean one shouldn't own a car.
Please do.
It is your money.
Enjoy it.
But don't confuse it with an asset.
It doesn't make money for you.

What about a house?
A house feels like an asset. You hope property prices increase.
But if you live in it and don't intend to sell it, it's not earning you money.
Instead, it takes money to run the house and makes you none.
Taxes, repairs, maintenance, loan EMIs.
Liability vibes, anyone?

But if you buy a house to rent out? That could be an asset, generating monthly income for you.

Your dominant goal with your money and time should be to build and buy assets.

Things that make you money.

That is when you make money work for you.

Ultimately, the biggest asset you have is yourself.
Your mind. Your body.
Your education. Your well-being.
Eat well. Exercise. Learn.
They open doors to new opportunities.
Invest in yourself.

For everything else:
Don't just look at the price tag.
See the full cost of ownership.
If it costs you money and loses value, it's a liability.

Aim to get assets that generate cash flow.
Assets that earn you money while you chill.
Assets that cover your expenses.
Assets that let you do the things you want to do.

Keep liabilities to a minimum.

Set up Multiple Income Streams. It's Not as Hard as You Think.

Think about what you really enjoy doing. Or what you're good at.
It could be investing or teaching.
Painting, singing, cooking.
Consulting or setting up a small business with friends or family.
Do it. Make money from it.

My job is super hectic. How do I find time for multiple streams?
It won't be easy to start out.
The voices in your head will tell you that you don't have the time. That it takes too much effort.
But who would you rather work hard for—yourself or someone else?

So, start.

First, stay in your current job.

Use your salary as a safety net.

This way, there's no pressure to make money off your other income streams from day 1.

Then take out time from your day job.

Early mornings, nights, weekends, holidays.

Devote that to building or buying assets.

The ultimate goal is to move towards a passive income stream—where you don't have to spend your time to make money.

Instead, your knowledge, your skill, your process, your money make money for you, through your assets.

What you are doing is using an existing skill (or developing a new skill) and then actively spending time to make money from it.

And then slowly begin to figure how to do the same without spending as much time.

Active income: Hustle and earn money for the time you put in	Passive income: Set up a system that keeps making you money with minimal time investment
» Pays you for the time you spend and the specific work you do. » You can have a side job, even if you have a full-time job. It's perfectly legal in India. » Just make sure your employment contract allows it (if you have a job). And that confidentiality isn't breached. » Can be converted to passive income after the initial set-up, if you use the right tools.	» A self-sustaining income stream. » Steady, regular income regardless of your active work hours. » Earn money while you sleep, literally. » Needs set-up and initial work. Once it gets rolling, minimum effort is required. » Passive income is your ticket to financial freedom. Make it count.

→ Take on Freelance Projects

Active income:

Use your skills.

Maybe you're a graphic designer. A writer. A web developer.

Maybe you're good at teaching. Baking. Cooking. Digital marketing.

Maybe you're multilingual, capable of translating!

Pitch these skills. Provide part-time services. Get paid.

Convert to passive income:

Start an agency.

Hire folks who do the same work that you have done so far.

Now they do the work.

Your time goes in organizing them, not in doing the work.

So even when you are not spending time, work is getting done.

→ Create Content

Active income:

Got a passion or an interest? Share it.

Choose your platform: start a blog, YouTube channel, social media account.

BE CONSISTENT.

Build an audience, engage with them. Authentic content always wins.

Convert to passive income:

Once your content gains traction, money follows.

Ads and sponsorships that earn you consistent money.

You can also earn through affiliate sales.

→ Online Courses

Active income:

Got expertise? Share it!

Host live classes.

You help others learn while you earn.

Convert to passive income:

Record the lessons once and run them as self-paced courses.

Upload them on platforms such as Udemy, Coursera, Skillshare.

Or perhaps on your own platform.

→ Invest in Stocks

Active income:

Do your research around stocks.

Technical analysis, fundamental.

Trade. Futures and options.

Be on the screen as soon as the market opens.

Convert to passive income:

Mutual funds—portfolio of stocks, managed by an expert for you.

You buy, they manage, you earn!

The performance of companies drives your returns over the long term.

→   Get on the Property Train

Active income:

Have a flat, room or even parking space?

Get smart with your space. Rent it out.

Might come with hassle—rent negotiation, collection, maintenance.

Some folks love it.

Some would prefer otherwise.

Convert to passive income:

Invest in real estate investment trusts (REITs) instead.

You can buy them just like stocks.

Your investments grow with the rental income they generate.

→   Earn through Royalties

Passive income:

Creative people, this one's for you!

Photographer: Sell photos on stock image sites. Earn per download.

Artist: License your artwork. Collect royalties for each sale/use.

Musician: Make music, earn royalties from songs being streamed.

Author: Write a book. Better still, an e-book. Collect royalties on each sale.

Tech professionals: Develop apps or software. Receive royalties on sales. Or sell the app.

The trick is to:

Try new things.

Stay curious.

It'll be tough to start, but, I promise you, it'll be so rewarding.

Personally and financially!

'Earn with your mind. Not your time.'

—Naval Ravikant

There's Enough for Everyone

Growing up, I thought that wealth was a zero-sum game. A finite 'pie'.
For someone to win, someone else had to lose.

We're conditioned to believe this.
It feels like there is nothing we can do about it.
A CEO's wealth comes at the staff's expense.
Our friend gets a good job; that's one opportunity less for us.

The reality is that there is no pie.
Wealth can be created, instead of just being distributed.

Imagine a Maggi packet. It costs ₹14.
Add water, toss in some veggies, serve with some ketchup—you've got a meal that's now sold for ₹45.
Someone added value and created wealth.

Wealth is not a zero-sum game, where the winner takes it all.
If someone won, it doesn't mean you will lose.
And for you to win, no one else has to lose.

There is space for everyone.
There is wealth for everyone.

Think about This

- Your salary is not enough. Think beyond it.
  There is no limit to how much you can earn.

- True wealth lies in acquiring real assets, not liabilities masquerading as assets.
  Most of us don't understand the difference between the two.
  Ask yourself: Does it earn you money?
  Yes? Asset.
  No? Possession. Maybe even a liability.

- Build a limitless mindset.
  Wealth is not a zero-sum game.
  One winner does not take it all.
  There's enough for everyone.

Do This

1. Reflect. Explore. Then identify 3–5 ways in which you can earn more money.
   Figure out *when* you'll start and *how* you'll start.

   _____

2. Think of the last thing you really wanted that made you say to yourself, 'Can't afford this.'
   Now, ask yourself, 'How can I afford it? How can I make it happen?'

   _____

SO THAT I CAN SPEND IT (WISELY)

'Singer Rihanna nearly went bankrupt after overspending.
She then sued her financial adviser.

'Adviser: Was it really necessary to tell her that if you spend money on things, you will end up with the things and not the money?'

—Morgan Housel,
The Psychology of Money

In 2016, my start-up faced a crisis.
Funds were depleting. People were laid off for no fault of their own.
Founders took pay cuts to save on cash.
My expenses were now higher than my income.

I continued spending as usual, thinking that money would come in soon. It didn't.
Maxed out my credit cards, borrowed from friends, because I needed money.
Not to survive. Instead, to maintain my lifestyle.

All because I thought that cutting down on my lifestyle was admitting failure.

But now I get it.
Spending money I didn't have, maintaining a lifestyle I couldn't afford: that was the true failure.

It's Not about Spending Less. It's about Spending Right.

The whole month you're hustling to earn money.
By the end of the month, the only thing you want
to know is where all your money went.
Bills. Rent. Other expenses.
You bought things that you really wanted.
You bought things that you didn't want at all.
It's all a blur.

And on the other side is the guilt.
Because the whole world's chanting, 'Save,
save, save!'

Here's the truth:
You can afford the things you love.
Actually, let me say it differently.
You SHOULD buy the things you love.
You SHOULD live the YOLO life, without the
stress.
Without the guilt.
No matter how much you earn.
What you need is discipline.

Budget your expenses.
It's like your financial Google Maps, getting you to your smart-spending destination.

Break down your income-after-tax:

- 50% on basic needs.
  A need is an essential expense that you cannot live without.
  E.g., rent money, EMIs, food, transport, phone/Internet bills, basic clothes, essential subscriptions.

- 30% on your wants/desires/things you love.
  Wants are the things you don't need but, instead, desire.
  These are the things you love, the things that make you happy.
  Weekend getaways. That fancy phone. Gadgets. Maybe a bike.
  Money to party or eat out.

- 20% on savings. To invest.
  So that you build for the future you.

And get to financial freedom at some point. More on this in the later chapters.

Let's assume your salary is ₹20,000 per month. Here's how you divide it:

Starting Salary	Needs	Wants	Savings
₹20,000 per month	₹10,000 (50%)	₹6000 (30%)	₹4000 (20%)

This rule is great when you've just started earning.
Do this for your first year. Or till you receive your first increment.

Once you receive an increment (or build an additional income stream), flip the 50:30:20 ratio.

- 50% of your increment goes to your investments
- 30% of your increment continues to go to your wants
- 20% of your increment goes to your needs

Let's say you add 10% to your previous income (through increments and side incomes), adding ₹2000 per month to your base salary of ₹20,000 per month.

Your salary will still be split using the 50 (needs): 30 (wants) : 20 (savings) rule.
The reverse ratio will ONLY be applied to your increments—50 (savings) : 30 (wants) : 20 (needs).

Like this:

Starting Salary	Increment	Needs	Wants	Investments
₹20,000		₹10,000 (50%)	₹6000 (30%)	₹4000 (20%)
	₹2000	₹400 (20%)	₹600 (30%)	₹1000 (50%)
New budget		₹10,400	₹6600	₹5000

In this way, you ensure 3 things:
1. Your needs do not grow with your income (which is a BIG mistake people make).
2. You keep building up the ratio towards your investments.

3. You still keep 30% for the things you love (wants).

Scan this QR code to download your own MS Excel budget calculator.

But why do I have to flip this ratio on every increment?
Why can't I keep it the same, 50:30:20?
Here's why:

-   So that your needs don't increase proportionally to your income.
    E.g.: *Your income jumps from ₹20,000 to ₹60,000 in 4 years. Does that mean you'll suddenly start eating triple the amount of momos you used to? Or hop on to 3 autos instead of 1 to reach the same destination? Nope! Your needs don't just shoot up from ₹10,000 to ₹30,000.*
    They'll grow as per inflation, while your total income may beat it!

- Your savings cannot remain at 20% of your total salary forever.
  Save more, so that you invest more.
  Invest more, so that you get financially independent soon.

This works irrespective of how much you earn.
Is your 'wants' budget ₹10,000 per month? And you want to buy a ₹25,000 phone?
Get a no-cost EMI option. Or wait for 3 months.
It fits in your budget.
Gets you disciplined about spending.

Forces you to cut your spending on the things you DON'T love and don't want, so you can spend on all the things you DO want.

'If you buy things you do not need, soon you will have to sell things you need.'

—Warren Buffett

Before You Spend, Pause. Ask Yourself This. Does It Make Sense for ME?

A weekend getaway with the gang? Sounds tempting.
There's also that phone you've been saving up for, and it's almost within reach.
But . . . beach, mountains, memories, right?
FOMO kicks in hard.

Take a pause.
Reflect on the 'why' before you 'buy'.

Is this trip genuinely for the joy, or is it about not wanting to be left out?
Always check: 'Is this something I really want, or do I just want it because everyone else wants it too?'

If it's what you want, adjust your finances and go ahead.
If not, say, 'Nah, not this time.'
FOMO and peer pressure make it tough to say no.

Even if it's beyond your budget.

What's the real cost?

Before you spend that money, check for hidden costs.

Those that are not upfront but lurking around somewhere.

Buying a new car?

The ex-showroom price tag is just the beginning.

Add costs you don't immediately see: registration fees, insurance, taxes, maintenance.

Plus, rising fuel costs, parking charges.

Buying a house?

You pay the price, and then the brokerage, registration, property tax.

Plus, the down payment, the interest on the loan.

And once you're in, the maintenance kicks in. The repairs.

Hey, maybe even your weekend getaway trip will have hidden costs—renting a car once you're there, the 1 beer that turns to 10.

Figure out the real cost.

Ramit Sethi, in his awesome book *I Will Teach You to Be Rich*, calls them 'phantom costs'.

You don't see them. You don't believe in them. Until you see them.

A Big Question: Buy or Rent a Home?

We're always told:
Home ownership = wisest investment decision +
ultimate life achievement.
Top-tier adulting.

Plus, the biggest logical justification:
If you are paying rent, you might as well pay
the EMI.
Right?
Well, not always!

Here's the unspoken truth:
When we decide to buy a home, it's almost
always an emotional decision.
We buy because we want to belong somewhere—
to put our names on that door.
We buy because we're afraid—that someday we
won't be able to afford the soaring rents.
We buy because we want security—to know
that we'll have a roof over our heads, no
matter what.

We buy because that's the only way we will get married—parents want financially well-off partners for their kids.

All valid.
But all emotions.
I'd argue:
Before you let emotions in, let your rational side take over.
Run the numbers first.
Because emotions will eventually come in, irrespective of anything else.

Introducing Rental Yield: A Cool Insider Secret
Rental yield = (annual rental you pay / property value) × 100

Picture this:
You rent a cute studio in Bengaluru.
Lovely society, top-notch amenities, 600 sq. ft.
House value? ₹1 crore.
Monthly rent? ₹20,000, incl. maintenance.

Rental yield math: You are paying 2.4% of the house value as rent, every year.
Yup, you are living the ₹1-crore life at 2.4% annual cost!

Imagine both the house value and the rent growing evenly.
Guess when you will end up owning that house?
After a whopping 40 YEARS of living there!

But let's break it down further.

Let's consider the costs associated with renting.
→ Key expense? Monthly rent.
It's like your ticket to live in a comfy space.
Minus the full-on commitment of buying.

Let's consider the costs associated with buying.
→ Down payment
It's a percentage of the property price you pay upfront.
Usually around 20–25% of the value.

It is a cost because if you can afford to spend this money, then you can afford to invest it as well.

But now, instead of earning returns on it, you make nothing off it.

That's an opportunity cost.

→ EMI (and interest)

If you take a loan, you have to pay EMIs every month.

It's like your new rent, but to the bank instead of the landlord.

And don't forget the interest.

For a ₹50-lakh home loan, you pay an additional ₹58 lakh as interest over a 20-year period.

WTF!

→ Registration costs

Think of it as putting your ownership in ink.

Varies between 3–7% of the home cost. And is paid by the buyer.

→ Brokerage fees

Brokers assist in your home search.

Their fee? The brokerage, a commission for their service.

Usually 1% of the home cost.

→ Maintenance costs

This is the home's upkeep bill.

From electricity to plumbing, it keeps everything running smooth.

It's the price you pay to keep your home a sweet home!

When you add up all these costs, you end up paying nearly 3X of the home price over a 20-year period.

Now, instead of buying at an early age, let's say you make 2 smart choices:

1. Invest the down payment for the next 10 years, as a lumpsum amount.

2. Invest the difference between what would have been your home loan EMI and the rent, as a monthly SIP (systematic investment plan).

Then, over a 10-year period you will build enough corpus to buy nearly 50–70% of your dream home on a down payment.

Don't trust me. Do the maths.

Scan this QR code to view the projections in an Excel sheet.

Don't get me wrong. I'm not saying don't buy a house.
Just don't buy it when you're young.

When you're young:
→ Renting offers a higher standard of living within your budget
Rental yields are very low in India (2–3%).
So your monthly rent is kinder on your wallet.
You might not be able to buy the posh apartment with a view.
But you can definitely rent it!

→ Renting frees up funds for investment opportunities

That down payment money? You can invest it elsewhere.

Stocks, bonds or even to start a side hustle.

This gives you a shot at growing your money.

→ Renting keeps life flexible

You're not tied down to one spot.

At least not early on.

Got a job opportunity in another city?

Want to explore different neighbourhoods?

Perhaps even move countries?

Renting lets you do it without the stress of selling a house.

It's like having a backpack instead of a suitcase.

You're ready to move whenever adventure calls.

Picture your early 20s.

You don't have a clue where you'll end up in a few years.

Renting feels like your passport to changing cities.
To changing jobs—all without being tied down.
Plus, let's face it—cash is always short.

Fast forward to your mid-30s.
You've got a clearer road map of where you want to be.
Settling down in a certain city? Buying starts to make more sense.
Financially, you've levelled up too.
That down payment money you invested in your 20s?
By now, it has grown to a respectable amount.
In your 30s, you're also more likely to be able to handle higher EMIs.
So, you pay less in interest over time.

The verdict: There's no one-size-fits-all answer.
My parents got their home at 50. I jumped in at 40.
When to buy? That's your call. Always.

Ultimately, only YOU can decide what's right for you.

Just make sure it's right for YOU.

Financially—run the numbers.

Emotionally—do it only if it brings you joy.

Stay Away from Bad Debt

Today, it's extremely easy to accumulate debt.
Easily available credit cards.
Tempting buy-now-pay-later schemes.

Bad debt is any loan that you take for a non-essential item or a depreciating purchase.
Car loans, credit card, consumer loans: potentially bad debts.

Did you know credit cards can hit you with a whopping 35–40% interest rate?
Compare that to the 8–9% on home loans. Or 10–12% on education loans.
Seriously, WTF?

Always pay off your credit card bill in full.

Don't fall for the 'minimum amount due' trap.
Your bank asks you to pay just 5–10% of the outstanding balance.
Sounds like a sweet deal, right? But the outstanding amount accrues interest. Your debt escalates.
Your due payment increases.

Plus, your credit rating is affected.

Credit cards give you the illusion of free money. You start thinking you're rolling in cash when you're really not.
It's like taking a loan while hoping you'll magically pay it off later.

Treat your credit card like a cool debit card. Swipe it only when you've got the cash ready to go.
Or when you're sure you'll have it next month.

Use credit cards to make you money!
→ Interest-free loans = free money
Credit cards offer a 30–45-day interest-free period.
Like a mini loan for whatever you need.
So if you make a big purchase using a card early in the month, invest that amount in a short-term debt fund.
You earn some happy money, for free!
Never say no to free money, my friend.

→ Improved credit score = easy, low-interest loan

Your credit score (CIBIL score) determines creditworthiness.

It increases based on how consistently you pay off your loans and how many loans you have.

Higher score = better credit profile.

So, if you pay your card bill on time and in full, your rating builds and improves.

Better rating means VIP-loan treatment in the future.

You get lower rates of interest!

And save money in the long run.

→ Reward points = freebies for you

Redeem reward points for air miles, free tickets, hotel stays.

Gift cards, cashback and more.

Explore and make the most of these freebies!

Pro tip:

When you apply for a credit card for the first time, opt for one with zero yearly charges.

If you can't get one, get one which is backed by a fixed deposit.

The Stress-Free Way to Clear Your Loans Faster

The ONLY principle you need to know: reduce the loan tenure.
So you can reduce the interest you pay.

Here's how you can pay off a 25-year loan in JUST 10 years:
Let's break down the loan basics.
EMI = principal (paid to clear the loan) + interest (paid to the bank).
In the initial phase: you pay more interest, less principal. Banks reap profits.
Over time: you pay more principal, interest declines.
The trick is to slash your interest costs as early as possible.

There are 2 ways to save interest on loans:
- Pay extra EMIs every year
- Keep increasing your EMI every year

Example:

Say you've taken a ₹40-lakh loan @ 8% for 25 years.

Every year: if you give 1 extra EMI (so 13 EMIs instead of 12) + increase your original EMI amount by 5% (every year)
You clear your 25-year loan in just 12.5 years!

What if you increase your EMI by 10% every year?
You'll clear your 25-year loan in JUST 10 years!
You will also save 50% in interest that you would have paid over 25 years.
The best part? It doesn't matter what the loan amount is.
This maths always works!

Let me repeat:
If you give 1 extra EMI every year + increase your original EMI by 10% every year, you pay off a 25-year loan in just 10 years!

Scan this QR code to see how it works in MS Excel.

Extra money in hand? Pay off loan or invest the money?
Check 3 things:

- Interest you're paying:
  - If >10%, then consider pre-paying, because the loan is expensive.
  - If <10%, consider investing the extra money in mutual funds. You can potentially earn a better return over a period of time.
- How old the loan is:
  - If it's more than 75% lapsed, do not pre-pay. Because in this case, you are paying more of the principal amount than the interest.
  - If it's less than 75% lapsed, consider pre-paying. You will save on interest.

- Outstanding amount:
    - If > extra cash, pay and reduce the term of the loan (not the EMI).
    - If < extra cash, pay in full and close the loan.

Severely in debt? Got multiple loans?

Two simple methods to handle them like a boss.

The 'Maths-Driven' Avalanche Method	The 'Win-Focused' Snowball Method
→ Rank the loans in decreasing order of EMIs.	→ Rank the loans in increasing order of EMIs.
→ Pay the highest EMI loans first, then move to the smaller ones.	→ Start with the smallest EMI loans first, then move to the bigger ones.
→ Since you will pay off the highest loans first, you will save a lot on interest.	→ Leaves you with a feeling of progress. It's like trying to lose weight. Seeing some movement on the scale gets you hyped to watch your diet and exercise. True for loans as well.
→ However, if the highest EMI loan is also a long-tenure loan, the process can be long and discouraging.	→ However, you pay more in interest overall.

Not sure which one to pick? Scan this QR code to test each method in MS Excel.

Bonus tips to pay off your loans faster:

→ Extend your loan duration

When you ask for more time, your monthly payments reduce.

Use the extra cash to pay the principal of young loans, where interest is still high.

→ Refinance expensive loans

Pay off high-interest loans first, then focus on the small fries.

For instance, ditch that hefty 40–50% credit card interest.

How? Swap it for a personal loan at 13–16%.

Use it to crush your credit card debt. Then, tackle the rest.

→ Keep loan instalments under 30% of income

Don't let it exceed this.

Stick with the 50:30:20 budgeting rule, and you will never misstep.

→ Settlement as the last resort

Negotiate a lower debt amount to clear your loan.

One major downside here: it permanently damages your credit rating.

Getting future loans becomes challenging.

'Pay off debt first.
Freedom from debt is worth more than
any amount you can earn.'

—Mark Cuban

Think about This

- Budget, budget!
  From your income after tax:
  50% goes to basic needs. 30% for wants/desires/things you love. 20% for investing.
  Flip the ratio on any increments/ side income you get.
  50% to investments. 30% to your wants. 20% for your needs.

  Budgeting forces you to distinguish between essential spending and discretionary spending.
  It encourages you to cut spending on things you DON'T love, so you can spend on all the things you DO.
  It compels you to save and invest, for your future.

- Before making any big money decisions:
  - Run the numbers.
    Consider ALL the costs associated, including the hidden ones.
    Check if it aligns with your long-term goals.

  - Do it only because YOU want to. Because it's right for you!
    Forget YOLO, FOMO and peer pressure when it comes to money.

- Don't get tangled in credit card debt—no minimum payments, please!
  Treat your credit card like a debit card. Swipe only when you have the cash.

Do This

1. Take stock. Of everything!

- Your yearly income
  Salary: _____
  Other forms of income (rent, side income, etc.): _____
  Interest earned (on FDs, etc.): ___
  Any other income: _____
  Total income: _____

- Your yearly expenditure
  Needs (EMIs, rent, utilities, travel, food, etc.): _____
  Wants (phone, eating out, travel, car/bike, etc.): _____
  Savings/investments: _____
  Total expenditure: _____

- Calculate the share of each expenditure category

Needs (divide needs by total spends): _____

Wants (divide wants by total spends): _____

*Savings (divide savings by total spends):*_____

Current proportion of needs: wants: savings (e.g., 50:30:20): _____

- Take stock of your bank accounts
  Note down how many bank accounts you have: _____
  Also how much money you have in each of them:

  _____

- Take stock of your debt
  Note down how many loans you have: _____

How much of the loan amount is due and how much time is left:

_____

Note down how many credit cards you have: _____

What is the outstanding amount on each card: _____

- Take stock of your investments

Write down all your investments so far and their approximate value.

Include gold, mutual funds, stocks, FDs, real estate, all of it.

_____
_____
_____
_____
_____
_____

You may not have all the exact numbers, but that's okay, approximations will do.
DO NOT let these numbers discourage you or encourage you. You're just figuring out your sh*t!

2. Understand your financial well-being.

• Calculate your total assets:

_____

This is a sum of all your investments and money, as of today.

• Calculate your total liabilities:

_____

This is a sum of all your outstanding loan amounts plus credit card bills.

• Figure out your net worth:

_____

That's (assets – liabilities).

3. Reflect
   Note down:
- Was it easy for you to figure out your financial data?

   _____

- Are you on the right track to where you want to be?

   _____

- What are the 3 things you're doing well? How can you do more of them?

   _____

- What are the 3 things you can improve on?

   _____

This is just a thinking exercise.
No judgement. No panic.
It's all good.

4. Act!
- Create a monthly budget sheet.  Scan this QR code for an easy budgeting tool in MS Excel. Use it to track how much you spend, save and invest. Start with at least 20% savings. As your income grows, ramp it up to 50%.

- Pay off your loans faster. Pay one extra EMI every year. Increase your EMI every year, say, by 10%. This reduces a 25-year loan to just 10 years!

- Clear your loans (especially the high-interest ones) as fast as you can.
  Refinance all credit card debt with a personal loan (it's much cheaper).
  Extend loan duration of old loans, to reduce their EMI. Use the extra cash to pay off young loans faster.
  Settle as the last resort. This dents your credit score forever, though.

BUT PEOPLE TELL ME I SHOULD SAVE!

*If you don't build the habit of saving
while your salary is small,
You'll never be able to save when you
begin to earn more.*

For 10 years, I took a below-market salary.
Instead, I opted for equity in my start-up.
Intentionally, I paid myself last.
Gambled on equity, but ignored savings.
Convinced it would give me much higher returns.

When things didn't turn out as expected, I was cash-strapped.
With barely enough to get by.

When I needed money the most, I found myself with the least.

Saving Isn't Sexy

We should save. We get it.
For the future, for our marriage, for our kids, for retirement.
Blah, Blah, blah. Heard it all before.

Yet, we don't.
Because saving isn't sexy. Or fun. Or exciting.
It's boring.

The future seems so far off.
Our goals seem so far off.
'Retirement? I haven't even started earning properly yet!'

AND we're not making enough money . . .
AND we'll miss out on life . . .
Our friends are putting up reels of sundowners in Goa.
Why should WE save?

So, we postpone saving.
We'll start tomorrow. Next month. Next year.
Just not today.

But We Should Save.

Because. Life. Is. Crazy.

Almost like a Bollywood movie.

One moment, we're happily dancing around a tree. Next moment, we're hit by a flying coconut.

Medical emergencies. Job losses.

Lawsuits. Unexpected death in the family.

Also. Because. We. Have. Dreams.

That house, that car, that fancy vacation, kid's education.

Plus our retirement one day.

Our money today has to pay for our desires tomorrow.

'Life will throw everything but the kitchen sink in your path, and then it will throw the kitchen sink. It's your job to avoid the obstacles.'

—Andre Agassi, *Open*

Savings Give You the Ultimate F***-You Power
The power to walk away from a job you hate.
The power to handle a medical emergency without depleting your reserves.
The power to get a better interest rate on a loan.
The power to move into your own place.
The power to live life on your terms.

You don't have to give up what you love.
Saving does not equal stopping spending.
Sitting at home. Being miserable.
Once you've decided how much you want to save, spend the rest on whatever you want.
With no guilt.

How Do I Start Saving?

Unless you know why you're saving, you don't know how much to save.

If you're just 'saving', it's a random number. If you don't hit it, you don't care.

So the drinks are always on you. You're always up for Zomato/Swiggy. Always ready to take that holiday.

There's nothing stopping you.

So, whatever you earn will always be little.

Whatever you spend, you'll always feel guilty.

Whatever you save and invest, you'll never know if it's enough.

You'll keep chasing money all your life.

But if you're 'saving for a vacation' or 'saving for a house', the goal gives you purpose.

It sharpens your decisions.

Reduces temptations. Brings focus.

Small difference. Big impact.

Set your goals. Know how much each one will cost.

→ List your goals. When do you want to achieve them?

- Long-term goals: Typically >10 years
  E.g., kids' education, retirement, down payment on a house.

- Medium-term goals: Typically goals you want to achieve in 3–10 years
  E.g., international vacation, further education, marriage, car.
- Short-term goals: <3 years.
  E.g., insurance, an emergency fund, a domestic holiday, a phone.

→ Figure out how much each goal will cost you.
  - Quote an approximate current price (ballpark) for each goal.
    The price won't stay the same forever, though.
    Because, inflation—the rate at which prices for goods and services rise over a period of time.
  - Calculate the 'future price' of your goal, based on the time frame you've set
    Assume an annual inflation rate of ~6%.
    E.g., your goal is to get married in 7 years. You need ₹10 lakh.
    Assuming 6% annual inflation, the final cost will be ~₹15 lakh.

RESULT:

	Goals	In how many years?	Current Cost	Future Cost?
Short term	Emergency fund	1	1,50,000	1,59,000
	Domestic vacation	2	50,000	56,180
	Mobile phone	2	50,000	56,180
Medium term	International vacation	4	2,50,000	3,03,754
	Education (MBA)	5	10,00,000	13,38,226
	Marriage	7	10,00,000	15,03,630
Long term	Home downpayment	15	20,00,000	47,93,116
	Kid's education	25	25,00,000	1,07,29,677
	Retirement	40	1,00,00,000	10,28,57,179

And then build the saving mindset.

→ Your target should be to save AT LEAST 20% of your salary.

Remember the 50:30:20 budget rule?

50% of your salary on your needs (essential spends).

30% of your salary on your wants (desires, because, hey, you have a life!).

20% of your salary on your savings (and thus investments—for your short-, medium- and long-term goals).

→ Save FIRST. Spend later.

    Most of us think that saving is income minus expenses. That's wrong.

    What if expenses go haywire one month? Does that mean you won't save?

    As soon as your income is credited, divert 20% to your savings.

    Automate that process—through SIPs, by sweeping it to a different bank account, whatever it takes!

Savings = Needs minus Ego.

Your needs: Rent, groceries, electricity and other can't-avoid-it essential bills.

Enter your ego: The new iPhone that you want, the Starbucks coffee you must have every day to look cool, those cool sneakers, the high-end gym membership, etc.

When you take out your ego expenses from what you're left with after your needs, that's savings.

Save first.

→ Don't just save. Invest.
  We were always told to save.
  But that, for most of us, meant keeping that money in a bank account.
  NO!
  We save to invest.
  Not to let the money rot in a bank account.
  These investments will generate returns to cover short/medium/long-term goals.

→ Where to invest is just as important as how much to save.
  Savings mean nothing if you do not invest wisely.
  That doesn't always mean investing where you get the maximum returns.
  It means understanding how different investments work for different goals. Mix and match to hit your goals.

We will cover this in detail in the chapter titled 'But What I Really Want Is to Grow My Money'.

Scan this QR code to download an MS Excel Budget Calculator that auto-generates this, based on the goals you set.

13 Tips to Help You Save More

→ Budget—boring but effective!
You can't improve what you don't measure.
Minimum 20% of your income has to be saved,
every month/year.

→ Automate your savings
If we have money in the bank, we tend to spend
it.
It's not always easy to do the right thing.
So, make the right thing easy!

Automate!

Sign up for as much EPF deduction as you can,
so it never reaches you.
Do monthly SIPs (and don't stop them!).
Open a separate investment account.
As soon as your salary hits, sweep your
investment amount to that account.

→ 30-day rule

If you really want to buy something big, wait for 30 days.

Chances are you'll decide you don't need it.

→ Try a fortnightly money 'fast'

Once a week or fortnight, don't spend on anything. Anything.

Spoiler: This will require some advance preparation.

Food? Take food from home.

Ride to work? Carpool.

Coffee? Your office coffee machine was made for this non-spending day.

→ Choose debit/UPI over credit cards

Debit/UPI is money you actually have.

Credit cards give you the illusion of money that you may not actually have.

If you don't have it, you can't spend it. Ha!

The best part? It's free (a lot of places still levy a surcharge on credit cards)!

→ Use credit cards, ONLY if you have 100% of the money

Credit cards can be a good thing:

- 30–45 days of an interest-free loan.
- Improved credit rating (if you make the full payment every month).
- Rewards and vouchers—who doesn't want those?

But ONLY IF you have the full amount.

→ Make shopping lists and stick to them

It's a fact—a list makes us stick to it.

Do this even if you're buying online.

→ Rent, if you're not a frequent user

Nowadays, everything is on rent—be it cars, gadgets or gowns!

So, don't buy things you won't use frequently.

In our parents' time, renting was shocking.

Today, the mantra is 'reduce, reuse'. Do that.

P.S. I rent my camera lens. The ones I like are insanely expensive, and I pay peanuts to use them for 7 days a year at most!

→ Buy bigger sizes

Bigger sizes tend to be cheaper, per unit.

If you have the storage space, buy larger packs, particularly non-perishable items.

→ Use deal/discount sites

Use deals and discount sites as much as you can. There's no shame in it.

It just means that you respect your money.

Your money will start to respect you back.

→ Pay off your loans faster

Early repayment saves on interest.

E.g.: Pay 1 extra EMI/year (13 instead of 12).

Increase that EMI by 10% every year.

A 25-year loan reduces to 10 years. And you save 60% on your interest amount!

Read about this in detail in the chapter titled 'So That I Can Spend It (Wisely)'.

→ Buy life insurance when you're young

You pay a lower premium and get longer coverage.

Why wouldn't you save on something so fundamental?

E.g., if you buy insurance when you're 25 till you're 65, you get 40 years of cover and STILL end up paying a lesser premium than if you were to buy the same cover at age 35 (and only get cover for 30 years).

Read about this in detail in the chapter titled 'And Use the Money to Protect Me'.

→ Shop online in incognito mode

Prices keep increasing when you keep searching for items online—flight tickets, hotels or even products.

Switch to incognito mode.

You'll get a price that is given to a new user.

This can't work on apps, so do your buying on your desktop or laptop.

Disclaimer: I have no way to prove this.

Use these hacks as a smart way to save more money, without compromising on your desires and needs.

Save as a gift to your future self:
The gift of security.
The ability to meet your life goals.
A safety net for unpredictability.
Freedom to live life on your own terms.

But.

DON'T go through life focusing only on a savings mindset.
There's a limit to how much you can save.
But remember, there's no limit to how much you can earn.
Keep finding ways to increase your income.
That will help you build wealth much faster than saving.

'If you don't design your own life plan, chances are that you'll fall into someone else's plans. And guess what they have planned for you?
Not much.'

—Jim Rohn

Think about This

There's always a limit to how much you can save.
Don't go through life skimping on things that matter.
Save and invest, but do so mindfully.
And focus on boosting your income.
Remember, that's limitless!

Do This

*   Set clear financial goals for yourself.
    What are the big expenses you expect in the short term (<3 years)?
    (E.g., new phone, vacation, new juicer, gym membership, etc.)

    _____

What are the big expenses you expect in the medium term (3–10 years)?
(E.g., further studies, new car, marriage, international vacation, etc.)

_____

What are the big expenses you expect in the long term (>10 years)?
(E.g., build a retirement fund, buy a house, kid's education, etc.)

_____

Calculate the money you need to meet those goals, according to today's price.

_____

Calculate the amount of money you need in life!

_____

This exercise is simpler than you'd think.

Scan the code below for a simple way to find your 'magic number' using an Excel sheet.

- Check: Are you saving at least 20% of your salary?
  If not, what are the steps you can take to increase your savings?

  _____

- Get that money out of your savings account and invest!
  Saving is meaningless without investing wisely.

AND USE THE MONEY TO PROTECT ME

'Insurance is like a parachute; if you don't have it the first time you need it, you won't need it again.'

—Unknown

At 26, I landed my first job.
Got health insurance from the company.
For myself and my parents. Yay!
The coverage was great. I was thrilled.

I left in 3 years to launch a start-up.
My corporate insurance lapsed. I delayed buying
a new plan.
BIG mistake.

One evening, my dad experienced excruciating
stomach pain.
He was diagnosed with severe pancreatitis.

After a week-long hospital stay, we saw the bill.
₹2.4 lakh!
I was shocked.
Stupid, stupid me.

First and Always . . . Protect Yourself

- Get health insurance to keep you steady amid surprise medical emergencies.
- Get life insurance for when the unimaginable occurs—death, disability, accidents.
- Build an emergency fund for everything else.

Let's start from the beginning.

Insurance:
A deal you make with a company to give you financial protection in case shit happens.
Think of it as a small token amount you pay to receive a huge sum of money, should you need it.

Premium:
The small token amount that you pay (every month or every year) to provide yourself with this safety net.

Cover:
The maximum amount you can avail, when the need arises or the event (for which you have taken insurance) happens.

Health Insurance: Protection against Surprise Medical Bills

Best age to get health insurance?

Your 20s.

Starting early is boss-level thinking. Here's why:

- Low premiums, high cover

Get this—when you're young and (hopefully) bossing your health game, your chances of hospitalization are lower.

So, insurance companies cut you a killer deal.

You pay less, and you get better cover.

- You get a no claim bonus

If you don't claim health insurance, many insurers reward you with a no claim bonus.

It's a discount or an increase in coverage that piles up over the years.

When you're younger, chances are high that you'll get the no claim bonus.

Because, hey, youth!

- Lower rejection rates
You're less likely to be rejected due to pre-existing health conditions.
As we age, health issues can arise.
Getting coverage while young ensures you're shielded from potential 'old people' problems.

How Do You Decide the Coverage You Need?

(Hospital days per year) x (hospital room rate)
Assume the number of days you might spend in a hospital per year.
A good personal ballpark is, say, 10–15 days.
Next, check the minimum hospital rate in and around your city, say, ₹25,000 per day.
Crunch the numbers: days multiplied by rate equals your tailored coverage.
In the example above: 10 days x ₹25,000 = coverage of ₹2.5 lakh.

For your parents, consider around 25–30 hospital days.
So, 25–30 days x rate = their coverage.

Family floater plan sounds like a sweet deal: Yes or no?

Not always.

Because the premium is decided based on the age of the eldest member.

Once your parents hit 60, their premiums will spike (because the probability of health issues is higher).

So, the family plan premium will also spike.

Parents also tend to clock in more hospital visits. They deserve a plan that's customized to their specific needs.

Here's a better approach:

One plan for you, your spouse and your kids.

And a different one for your parents.

What if you're already sorted with corporate health insurance?

You STILL need personal cover. Here's why:

- When you switch jobs, your corporate cover ends.

So does your no claim bonus—all that healthy living for nothing.

Plus, the waiting period for pre-existing diseases (PEDs) is reset. It starts all over again.

In India, you can have 2 health insurance plans at once.

For cashless payments, only one plan can be used at a time.

After the cashless bit, you can use the second plan for the remaining expenses.

For instance:

Hospital bill: ₹4 lakh

Corporate plan: ₹2 lakh

Personal plan: ₹3 lakh

Use ₹3 lakh from your personal plan for cashless payment.

Pay ₹1 lakh in cash, then claim reimbursement from your corporate plan.

- Most corporate plans have a co-pay option It's like splitting the medical bill with the insurance company.

You usually chip in around 10–20% of the cost.
The company handles the rest.
It's meant to avoid misuse.
With personal insurance, there is no co-pay.

-    Might not include all treatments or procedures
Corporate insurance plans might skip specific medical treatments or procedures.
They are the same for all employees, irrespective of their needs.
With a personal plan, you're in control, tailoring your coverage to match your requirements.
No compromise, no shortcuts—just the protection you need.

Top 3 Things to Look Out for in a Health Insurance Plan

-    Pre-existing disease (PED) coverage

Make sure your plan covers past health issues.
Then, check the wait time: How long do you have to wait for PED coverage?
Around a year is okay, any longer is not.

- No room rent limit

Pick a plan that doesn't put a cap on room costs. You deserve the freedom to pick your room, without stress about extra expenses.

- Cashless hospital network

Look for plans linked to hospitals that offer no-cash bill settlement.

Check how many such hospitals are nearby to avoid long drives during emergencies.

How to Buy Health Insurance?

First off, buy directly/online and NOT through insurance agents—they've got their sneaky commissions built into the cost, making your policy more expensive.

A good place to buy is PolicyBazaar. They've got all the plans lined up for you to choose from, making it as easy as ordering pizza.

It's like the MakeMyTrip or ixigo of the insurance world.

If you're completely clueless, you can choose the services offered by Ditto Insurance.

They offer unbiased consultation tailored to your needs.

Sadly, none of these companies are paying me anything for this shout-out.

And here's a pro-tip: If you already like a specific insurance company, go straight to their website and make the purchase.

Life Insurance: Protection for the Fam

Life insurance is an old-people thing? NO!
Just like health insurance, getting your life insurance when young means lower premiums.
Early bird FTW!

The sweet spot: From 25 to 35. You get the right blend of coverage and cost.
Buy it till your retirement—think long term.
If you're 25 and will retire at 65: take a life insurance plan for 40 years.

It's a safety net for your loved ones, especially if you're the main provider.
In case (God forbid) something happens to you, they won't be left in a tough spot.
They'll have the financial backing to continue their lives.

The 3 Main Plans You Need to Know About

- Term plan: Low premium, highest coverage

It provides coverage for a set period of time: 10, 20, 30 years and so on.

You pay an annual premium to the company.

In the event of your death, your family gets a payout.

If you stay healthy till the term ends, you get nothing.

Sounds like a waste of money.

But, wait . . .

- You get MAX COVER at the MINIMUM PREMIUM since the company owes you only in the event of death.

    As of 2023, you pay approximately ₹11,000 per year for a ₹1-crore cover, if you're around 25 years of age.

- You pay a steady annual premium, but its real value declines over time (it's getting cheaper for you).

    How? The rising cost of living caused by inflation.

The value of the ₹11,000 will feel like ₹6000 a year when you're 35; ₹3500 a year when you're 45.

- The premium qualifies for a tax deduction under Section 80C.

- Investment plan: Blends insurance and investment

You pay some part for the insurance cover. The rest is invested—stocks or bonds.

In the unforeseen event of your death, your family gets the cover amount AND the investment amount.

If you continue to live and the policy matures (it finishes its term), you get the investment amount.

What will the investment amount be? It depends on where you chose to invest.

That's awesome. Why do people even consider a term plan then?

Because:

- Premiums are higher for the same cover, because, hey, you're getting something back at the time of maturity.
  The same ₹1-crore plan with investment returns will cost you around ₹20,000 per year.
- The returns aren't always very attractive. You might make better returns investing by yourself.

- Guaranteed return plan: High premium but guaranteed payout

Picture it like a savings account, but with extra benefits.

You put in money.

In case of your death, your family gets the cover amount PLUS the investment amount.

When the plan ends, you get a guaranteed amount or a guaranteed return.

It's always more than what you gave: depending on the plan, duration of investment, interest rates, etc.

For example, a ₹1-crore life insurance plan that returns your premium back to you on maturity will cost ₹30,000 per year.

At the end of 60 years, you will get approximately ₹25 lakh.

Which will seem like a lot.

But remember: the money you get back will not have the same buying power as today.

Because? You guessed it: inflation!

How Do You Decide How Much Coverage to Take?

Make sure it's at least 10 times your annual salary—ideally, 25 times.

So, if your annual salary is ₹5 lakh per annum, then take a cover of at least ₹50 lakh and, ideally, ₹1.25 crore.

What Are Add-Ons and Why Should You Care?

Think of them as your personal boosters.

They make the plan personalized to fit your unique needs.

Top 4 add-ons you should definitely consider:
→ Critical illness add-on
If you're hit with a major illness and can't work, this add-on gives you a payout to keep you afloat.

→ Disability add-on
Say you can't work due to a disability. This add-on steps in with a payout to keep things steady.

→ Premium waiver on critical illness
If critical illness strikes, future premiums are put on pause.
You get to focus on your recovery.

→ Premium waiver on disability
If you're disabled, this add-on waives off your premiums.
Your coverage is kept intact.

How Do You Pick the Right Life Insurance Company to Partner With?

→ Brand reputation
Choose a company with a solid track record.

Life insurance is a long-duration product, so bet on brands you trust.
Reputed brands. Maybe even your banking partner.

→ High claims ratio
Check the claims ratio: When people claim insurance, what percentage is actually processed?
Higher number of claims is a good sign.
Look for at least 99%.

→ High payout ratio
Check the amount paid out as a ratio of the amount claimed.
When people claim insurance, what percentage of the value claimed is actually paid?
A higher payout ratio is a good sign.
Again, at least 99%.

When you get a life insurance policy, disclose EVERYTHING.

Lay it all out there—smoking, health history, lifestyle choices.

Full disclosure keeps your coverage rock solid! Leaves no room for insurance companies to dodge or deny payments later.

How to Buy Life Insurance?

First decide what kind of plan you want—term, investment or guaranteed return plan.

My recommendation would be term insurance.

Just as with health insurance, buy directly/ online and NOT through an agent.

The latter has a commission built in, making it more expensive.

Good places to buy from—PolicyBazaar, Ditto. They haven't paid me for saying this, in case you are once again wondering!

If you know which insurance player you want to partner with, you should ideally go directly to their site and buy.

Emergency Fund: Protection against Everything Else

Health emergencies? Covered.
Family protection? Covered.
Now, an emergency fund? Seems a bit extra.

Imagine you're in your early 20s, making ₹25,000–30,000 a month.
Life's cruising along, when bam!
You're hit with an unexpected ₹1-lakh expense.
Now what? A loan might seem like an easy fix.
But let's face it, it's not always the most reliable option.
Plus, who wants to start their 20s tangled up in EMIs?
That's where an emergency fund comes in.

Emergency fund is like a DIY insurance plan.
Cash hidden away for the events that life and health insurance can't cover.
Car breakdowns, home fixes, sudden job jolts, legal surprises, travel emergencies.
The unexpected stuff.

How Much Do You Allocate to Your Emergency Fund?

→ Break down your monthly must-pays

Rent, EMIs, utility bills—the essentials.

→ Multiply them by 6

Voila! You've got a 6-month safety stash to start with.

Want to be extra prepared? Aim for a 12-month cushion—that's ideal.

3 easy ways to build your emergency fund

→ Hit pause on spending sprees and investments for a bit.

Your emergency fund takes the front seat for now.

→ Unexpected windfall? Whether it's a bonus, money from a parent or a matured FD, dump it straight into your fund.

→ Create a designated account—separate or as a sub-account—for the fund.

Rain or shine, drop in your contribution each month.

Where Do You Keep the Emergency Fund?

→ Set aside 10% as actual cash—immediate access

Makes it easy to grab funds ASAP.

→ Allocate 20% to your bank account—access in hours

Opt to keep it in a savings account.

Yes, it only earns 3–4% on an average per year, but this money is not for growth. It's for emergencies.

→ Park the remaining 70% in fixed income funds—access in 24–48 hours

Could be a fixed deposit. Yes, an FD! There, I said it.

You're not looking for growth. You just need something that allows for free and fast withdrawal, without any penalty.

Or a debt mutual fund.

Pro Tips

- Emergency fund first, investments later.
- Keep it bulletproof—no stock adventures, no crypto escapades, no gold or real estate experiments. Use the fund ONLY for real emergencies, not for impulsive buys.
- If you tap into your fund, refill it ASAP.

'An emergency fund is like insurance for your peace of mind.'

—Dave Ramsey

Do This

- Get health insurance
  One surprise medical emergency can wipe out your entire life's savings. So, be prepared!
  Your 20s are the best time: you pay low premiums and get a no claim bonus.
  - Do your research first!
  - What coverage amount is best for you?
  - What are the absolutely non-negotiable things your plan needs to cover?
  - Do you have health insurance for you, your spouse and kids?
  - Do you have health insurance for your parents?
  - Do you have separate insurance from your corporate insurance?

- Get a separate policy for you and your family, and a separate one for your parents.
- Get a personal health insurance plan even if you have corporate health insurance.

- Get life insurance

  Your mid-20s are the best time to get this done because of the lowest premium.

  Term insurance is the best form of insurance, in my opinion.

  - Do your research (always)!
  - What coverage amount is best for you?
  - What are the add-ons you need?
  - What type of life insurance plan is best for you?

- Build an emergency fund
  Get a 6-month fund, minimum.
  Ideally, a 12-month fund.
  Split the fund: 10% cash; 20% bank
  account; 70% in fixed income.
  Use the fund ONLY for real
  emergencies, not for impulsive
  buys.

BUT WHAT I REALLY WANT IS TO GROW MY MONEY

'Investing should be like watching paint dry or watching grass grow.
If you want excitement, take $800 and go to Las Vegas.'

—Paul Samuelson

I assumed that only wealthy people invested.
Only they could afford it.
Only they had the surplus to invest.

So, for years, I avoided investing.
Once I made more money, then I would invest.
Maybe a huge bonus or payout.
Then I would invest.

I wish I'd known that we don't have to be wealthy to invest.
It's the other way around—we need to invest to get wealthy.

I missed my opportunity to take advantage of the power of time.

I waited too long. You shouldn't.

Earning Gives You Financial Stability. Investing Gives You Financial Independence.

When we get a job, we assume that we're financially independent.
We get money regularly. We can pay for what we need.
We're set up for life.

But are you?
You're dependent on that job for money.
Job ends = income ends.
Earning gives you financial stability.
It doesn't give you financial independence.

True financial independence comes:
When income from your investments pays for your needs and expenses. For life!
When you work because you want to, not because you have to.
When you have money to live well, even without the 9-to-5 grind.
That's financial freedom.

We waste our lives obsessing over money.
If we learnt how to invest right, we could focus on living more and worrying less.

Investing Isn't What You Think It Is

Investing isn't what we see in movies.
Those hectic trade floors. Rapid-fire decisions.
High stakes. High tension. Heartbreaking losses.
Instant millionaires! Instant paupers!

We think that investing is about quick gains.
In reality, it's a slow climb. A steady progression to build wealth over time.

We think that investing is about waiting till you have 'more money to play with'.
In reality, it's not about how much you invest, but when you start investing. Seriously!
If you invested ₹500 a month in the stock exchange at the age of 20, by the time you are 60 you would have 60 lakh.

If you invested ₹500 a month, starting 30, by the time you are 60, you would have only ₹17.6 lakh.

EVEN if you invested ₹1000 a month starting 30, by the time you are 60, you would have only ₹35 lakh.

See the power of investing early?

We think that investing is too risky.
In reality, all choices have risks.
Keeping your money in an FD or savings account carries a risk.
It's called inflation risk.
The value of your money erodes every year, because it's not even beating the rate of inflation.

Saving is great, but it's pointless without investing.
The biggest risk is taking no risk.

Every Good Investor Was Once a Beginner

Invest early. Invest consistently.
Because compound interest is awesome.

Compound interest is every single reason why we're told to invest early and to invest consistently. Because, with compound interest, your money earns money on its own.
You earn interest on interest!
Without ANY work!

It works like this:
You invest ₹20,000 in a mutual fund with a 10% rate of return.

Year 1
Investment: ₹20,000
Rate of return: 10%
Returns earned: ₹2000
Your total investment now: ₹22,000

Year 2
New investment base: ₹22,000
Rate of return: 10%
Returns earned: ₹2200

Hang on a minute. Did you see what just happened?

Your return isn't the ₹2000 you earned on your original investment.

It is now ₹2200.

So, you're not just earning on your original amount, you're also earning interest on your interest!

FML!

Your total investment now: ₹24,200

Year 3
New investment base: ₹24,200
Rate of return: 10%
Returns earned: ₹2420 (compared to ₹2200 the previous year and ₹2000 the first year)
You see what's happening?

*EVERY YEAR, YOU'RE EARNING MORE
THAN LAST YEAR FOR THE EXACT SAME
RATE OF RETURN!*

In 3 years, you earn ₹6620!

*In 10 years, you'll have ₹51,875. That's over
double your investment.*

In 45 years, you'll have ₹14.6 lakh.

Without doing anything.

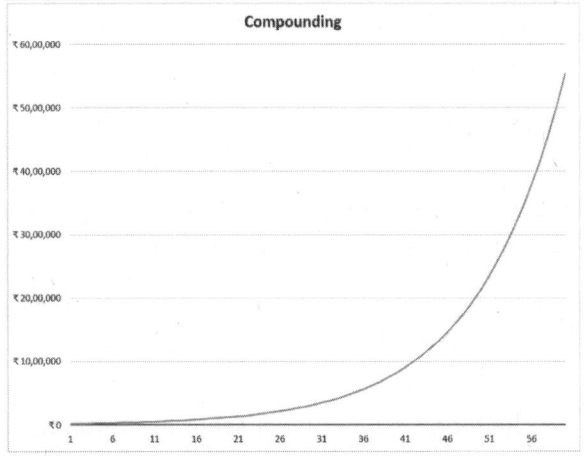

You didn't put in any more money.

The growth rate remained the same.

BUT you earned interest on your interest.

Every year, your base (on which you earned interest) grew.
Year after year, your money compounded.

Compounding rests on time.
Early on, the curve seems almost flat.
But after that, whoosh!

In the scenario described, you didn't put in another rupee after the initial ₹20,000 investment.
You still doubled your investment in 10 years.
Imagine how quickly you can take advantage of compounding if you keep contributing to your investment monthly or even annually!

Allow compounding to happen.
It takes time. Decades.
For the longest time it will seem like nothing is happening.
But it IS happening!

'Compound interest is the eighth wonder of the world. He who understands it, earns it.'

—Albert Einstein, *apparently*

All we need is time.
Start early.

Picture this:
You and your friend.
Both 25
Same job, same ₹6 lakh/year salary.

You save 20% of your salary right away. That's
₹1,20,000 per year, or ₹10,000 per month.
Invest it in a mutual fund, 12% annual returns.

And then you meet your friend when both of you
are 45.
You're sitting on, guess how much?
A cool ₹1,00,00,000.
Yes—that is a cool crore, my friend! Really!
Beautiful, beautiful, compounding!

Your friend had a different journey, though.
He laughed at you for investing 20% of your
salary in your 20s.
That's the age to enjoy and live life, baby!
So that's what he did.

Spent his money on things.
Trying to impress people.

And then, at 35 he decided to beat you at your own game.
At that point, both of you are earning ₹12 lakh per annum.
And he says, I am not going to invest just 20%.
I am going to invest 30% of my income!
That is, ₹3.6 lakh per year, or ₹30,000 per month.
3X your monthly investment.

He meets you at 45.
And he has ₹70 lakh.
70% of what you have, with 3X your monthly investment.

He invested more.
But he started later.
So he ended up with less.

Your 20s may seem like the worst time to invest.

Your bank balance? Not where you thought it should be.
Education loans? Ugh.
Random expenses? They just keep coming.
Feels like you're always short.

Your 20s are actually the BEST time to start investing.
Absolute prime time.
Every good investor is about that edge.

You don't need to be the next Wolf of Wall Street.
You don't need super stock-picking powers or secret skills.

Because you have the ultimate cheat code: TIME.
That's your VIP pass. Your greatest asset.

Start. Let your money compound.

We Also Need Returns . . . with Minimal Risk!

We love returns!

Every time we invest, we picture the potential gains.

Yet, with every potential reward, there's an inherent risk.

The new crypto that's all over your feed? It could soar or crash overnight.

That trending stock? Could skyrocket or tank.

That cutting-edge start-up? Huge potential but could stall before taking off.

Risks can't be eliminated. But they can be managed.

Lower risk typically means lower returns.

Think FDs. Low risk, but returns barely beat inflation.

Higher risk could mean higher returns or higher losses.

Think crypto. Potentially huge gains. Potentially huge losses. It's a casino!

Your risk tolerance influences how you invest.

High risk tolerance → you could overreach

Low risk tolerance → could mean missed opportunities

Super-low risk tolerance → could mean you don't want to invest at all!

Finding that balance is the sweet spot.
Maximum rewards for a chosen risk level.

Enter Asset Allocation

Asset allocation spreads investments across different asset classes (or, put simply, different things to invest in), to balance risk and return.
Different assets perform differently at various times.
If one asset is doing poorly, another might be doing well.

By investing across multiple asset classes:
-   We shield against unexpected losses in any one asset class.

- We tap into higher growth opportunities than if we invested in just one asset class.

An optimal portfolio tries to give you that balance.
It maximizes returns for a set risk. Or minimizes risk for desired returns.

Understanding Various Asset Classes

1. Low Risk

1.1 My parents say invest in fixed deposits

Bottom line:
As a protection tool (e.g., to park emergency funds), an FD works well.
As an investment tool, think beyond FDs.
Please.

We click and swipe. For everything.
To read. Learn. Buy. Travel. Eat.
Even to find love.

Still, somehow, with money, we're super traditional.

We LOVE fixed deposits!

We imagine our hard-earned money stored in an iron vault, in the bank down the road, guarded by top security—no harm can ever come to it. Feels super safe. Risk-free.

Is your money secure? Quite likely.
Is it growing? Let's see.

Consider this:
FD returns are currently ~6%
Invest ₹100 in an FD, get ₹106 at the end of the year.
But, inflation also averaged 6% in India from 2012 to 2023.
What costs ₹100 will cost ₹106 in a year.
Which means, your actual returns, after adjusting for inflation, are 0 (that's ZERO).
Add taxes (that you have to pay on the interest earned of your FD) to that and your actual returns are negative.

If you're keen on an FD anyway:

- Use an FD as a protection tool (think: a place to park your emergency funds), rather than as an investment tool to grow your funds.

Check that the bank waives off the penalty fee in case of early withdrawal for emergencies.

- If you already have an FD (I knew it!), use it to get an FD-linked credit card.

Start building a good credit score.

Make the FD work for you!

How to invest in an FD: Buy from a bank, preferably a nationalized one.

Fixed deposits: where your money enjoys a steady relationship with interest, and they never break up.

1.2 The government tells me PF and NPS.

Bottom line:
EPF (employee provident fund) and PPF (public provident fund)—the government's dynamic duo to set you up for the future.
EPF is for the salaried; PPF is for everyone.
You're salaried and need to choose between EPF and PPF? Consider EPF.
Top up with NPS (National Pension Scheme) for that market edge.

Flashback:
Ever dreamt of a government job?
Guaranteed pension = happy retirement.

These schemes are the alt-route to a happy retirement—for the private-sector peeps, the self-employed and unemployed!

NPS, PPF and EPF—here's what they have in common:
- Government-established.
- Sweet tax benefits.

-    They play the long game:
They're not your impulse-buy funds.
Instead, think future goals and retirement money.

Employee Provident Fund (EPF)

A long-term savings scheme for salaried folks.
-    You pitch in part of your salary, your employer matches it and voila—into the EPF it goes.
-    For companies with >20 employees, this isn't a choice. EPF is mandatory.

Here's a simplified version of an EPF calculation:

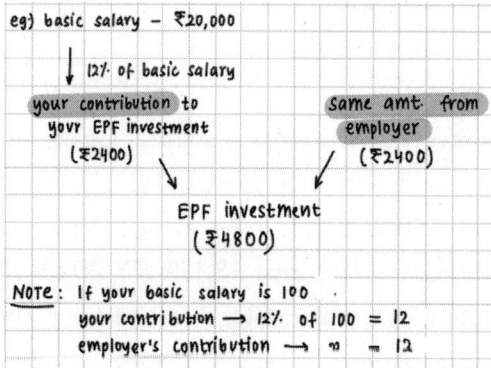

eg) basic salary — ₹20,000

↓ 12% of basic salary

your contribution to your EPF investment (₹2400)

same amt. from employer (₹2400)

EPF investment (₹4800)

NOTE: If your basic salary is 100
your contribution → 12% of 100 = 12
employer's contribution → " = 12

→ Your CTC = ₹112 (₹ 100 + employer contribution)
→ Your take home = ₹88 (₹100 − your contribution)

EPF deduction:
- Salary <₹15,000/month?
  EPF deduction = 12% of basic salary

- Salary >₹15,000/month?
  <u>Option 1</u>: Invest 12% of ₹15,000, the minimum investment amount.
  That's ₹1800/month.

  <u>Option 2</u>: Invest 12% of your monthly basic salary.
  I'd ask you to consider this option—future you will thank you!

Why bother?
→ Forces you to invest regularly. Consistently. That makes wealth-building easy.
→ As risk-free as any investment can be.
→ Guaranteed returns: ~8.15% (FY 2023–24).
→ Potential tax benefits, if you're filing under the old regime.

EPF withdrawal:
- Currently working?
Nope, can't touch the EPF stash.

- After 2 months of resigning you can withdraw all the money from your PF account.
    - Worked <5 years?
      TDS is deducted @ 10% on EPF balance if the amount is above ₹50,000.
      Exceptions for specific cases—if your employment ends due to ill health,
      your employer's business shuts down or withdrawal reasons are beyond your control.
    - Worked > 5 years? No taxes.

- Switching jobs?
  Transfer that EPF from the old company to the new.
  Let's say you've worked for 3 companies over the past 7 years.
  If you're withdrawing it after 5 years, you still don't pay tax.

Doesn't matter, whether you're working with employer 1, 2 or 3!

<u>How to invest in EPF</u>: Through (and with) your employer!

Public Provident Fund (PPF)

Designed for those not clocking in a salaried 9-5.

- Think less than 20-member start-ups, freelancers or even those chilling post retirement.
- All Indians are welcome (unless you're an NRI).
- Because it's so non-discriminatory, returns are less than those of EPF.
- If you do have a choice between EPF and PPF, consider opting for EPF.

How does it work?

- Open an account via a bank's website, or by going to a bank branch or post office.

- Every year, a minimum of ₹500 and a maximum of ₹1.5 lakh can be invested in PPF.
- You can invest annually or quarterly.

Why bother?
→ Potential tax benefits if you're filing under the old regime.
→ A good low-risk option for your portfolio— definitely better returns than most FDs!
→ Guaranteed returns: 7.1% (FY 2023–24), adjusted annually by the government.
→ Loan option: You can borrow against your PPF, between the 3rd and 6th year.

Withdrawal of PPF:
PPF has a 15-year term. Extensions possible in 5-year blocks.
Permits partial withdrawals from year 7.
Emergency withdrawals: specific to certain limits and time periods.

<u>How to invest in PPFs</u>: Open your PPF account in a bank or post office. Online or offline.

National Pension System

A government-backed pension scheme.

- Open to all Indian citizens, between the ages of 18 and 70. Includes NRIs.
- Retirement-oriented saving scheme.
- Unlike EPF and PPF, NPS is a market-linked product—your money is invested in a mix of equity, government debt, corporate debt and alternative assets.

  Think of it as a mixed mutual fund, where part of your money is invested in debt and part of it in equity.

How does it work?

- Register via the eNPS online platform.
- Minimum initial contribution to invest: ₹500.
- Minimum investment: ₹6000/year.

Why bother?

→ Additional source of avenue to save money for a retirement income.

→ You have a say in how your money will be invested.

Lets you choose the distribution between equity funds, government securities fund, fixed income instruments and other government securities.

→ Potential tax benefits under the old regime and the new regime.

NPS offers Tier-1 and Tier-2 accounts.

Tier 1: the principal NPS account for building a retirement fund.

Your money is locked in till the age of 60.

Potential tax exemptions under both the old and new tax regimes.

You get the maturity amount on retirement (when you're 60):

- 60% as a lump sum. This is not taxable.
- 40% every month, like a monthly salary. It's taxable as per your income tax slab.

Tier 2: a voluntary savings account.

It's an add-on to the Tier-1 account.

No lock-in period—its main value is to offer flexibility in withdrawals and exit.

No tax deductions. Corpus is taxed on exit.

How to invest in NPS: Through the eNPS website.

Investing in PF/NPS is like planting a money tree that only blossoms after retirement. The more you nurture it now, the more shade it will provide later.

1.3 Grandparents say gold.

> Bottom line:
> Do not invest in jewellery.
> Instead, invest in sovereign gold bonds.
> They pretty much check every box on the 'top
> 3 reasons people invest in gold' checklist.

→ Jewellery

Buy jewellery if you like. Probably best not to think of it as an investment, though!

(+)	(−)
- An easy way to start investing in gold. - Great because you can wear it! - Kill it at weddings and parties. Dazzle 'em all!	- 10–30% making charges (over and above the cost of the gold). - ~3% GST on ready-made jewellery - Need for secure storage—often inconvenient and costly. - Purity isn't always assured.

→ Gold bars/gold coins:

An easy way to invest in gold. Maybe not the smartest way.

(+)	(–)
- No making charges! - Guaranteed purity. - Quality assured by hallmark.	- Can't wear those bars around your neck. - 3% GST. - Cost of secure storage.

<u>How to invest in gold bars/gold coins</u>: Buy from a reputed 'brand', your trusted family jeweller or MMTC-PAMP.

→ Digital gold

Your beloved, beloved, gold. Just stored digitally.

Physical gold's cooler, more modern cousin.

Each bit you buy is stored in a certified vault in your name.

P.S. in case you're wondering, you don't need a demat account.

(+)	(−)
- Transparent—buy/sell at real-time market rates. - No storage problems for you! - Guaranteed purity. Cash out when you like. - Invest from as low as ₹100, or ₹1!	- It's digital, so no shiny things to flaunt daily. - 3% GST. - ~2–3% platform commission. - Keep it too long (>5 years) and you'll pay storage fees.

How to invest in digital gold: Buy from MMTC-PAMP or a reputed digital gold platform.

Or buy through 'brand' jewellers who have tie-ups with such companies.

Or buy through platforms such as Paytm, Google Pay or PhonePe, which have tie-ups with these companies.

Or buy through fintech companies such as Groww and 5paisa.

So many options. They're making it really easy for you!

→ Sovereign gold bonds (SGBs)
Government-backed digital gold bonds.

(+)	(−)
- 100% secure. - Buy it online, easily. - Guaranteed purity. - Low minimum investment: 1 gram of gold. - Growth in value + 2.5% annual returns on the value invested. *The 2.5% returns are accrued (added to your principal every year).* - Tax benefits: No capital gains tax if held until maturity, i.e., 8 years.	- Only for Indian residents (sorry, NRIs!). - Available in specific periods (when the RBI says so!). - Longish maturity period—8 years. - 20% capital gains tax if redeemed after 5 years (with indexation). - Max 4 kg per person.

How to invest in SGBs: Issued by the RBI, SGBs can be bought through offices, branches or net-banking sites offered by nationalized banks, scheduled private banks and scheduled foreign banks.

Think SBI, ICICI Bank, HDFC Bank, Canara Bank, Axis Bank, Bank of Baroda.

Also, via designated post offices, StockHolding Corporation of India Ltd (SHCIL).

→ Gold mutual funds
Mutual funds that invest mainly, or only, in gold. Gold mutual funds are bought or sold at the current net asset value (that's the price per unit of the fund).

(+)	(−)
- Flexible investment amount (minimum of ₹1000). - Buy/sell on short notice and without hassle. - Allow for SIP investments. - No inconvenience of storage.	- You don't actually own gold. - Cost of 0.6–1.2% of your investment. - Possible exit load (penalty) in the range of 1–2% if you redeem before a year.

<u>How to invest in gold mutual funds</u>: Buy directly through the mutual fund company or through platforms like Zerodha (Kite), Groww, Angel One, Upstox, ICICI Securities, etc.

Investing in gold is like having a shiny pet rock. It doesn't fetch, roll over or do tricks, but it has a way of making you feel richer.

2. Medium Risk

2.1 Corporate uncle says corporate bonds.

> Bottom line:
> You lend to companies, they promise to return your principal plus guaranteed interest.
> If the bond is thoroughly vetted, it can be a win-win!

Businesses always need funds.
To scale up, expand operations, buy new equipment, build new facilities. Grow!
One way of raising these funds is by issuing a bond.

When you buy a bond, you're lending to that company.
In return, they commit to pay back with interest.
Think FDs—but this time you are lending.

E.g., you invest ₹1000 in a 10-year bond at 9% interest.

That's ₹90 in your pocket every year and the original ₹1000 back after a decade.

The good part:
- Guaranteed return rates—no volatility.
- It has nothing to do with the equity market. So, stock market mood swings don't dictate your returns.
- Regular, predictable stream of interest payments on set dates.

The not-so-good part:
- Tracking the company can be like deciphering a puzzle.
  Understanding profits, growth, leadership shifts, how the money is used!
  As a retail investor, you try, but never quite succeed, in piecing it together.
- Defaults are real.
  Sometimes, the company may not be in a position to repay in a timely manner.
  Or repay at all.
  That's 100% of your money gone!

This 'default risk' makes the company's creditworthiness—its ability to meet its debt obligations on time—an important concern for bondholders.

Here's where credit rating agencies (CRAs) come in.

They size up companies and projects.

Dole out ratings.

From AAA, AA, A, BBB . . . all the way down to a C and a D.

AAA, AA and A are considered great bonds to invest in. Investment grade, they call it!

AAA is top-notch. The CRA fully expects that you would get back the money as promised.

AA is brilliant. A holds its own.

B bonds, though, are a bit iffy. They come with more risk.

So why would anyone invest in a C? Or worse, a D?

Risk and reward.

These (appropriately called junk bonds) have greater risk, but they can also offer you greater returns.

Only if things work out, obvs!

Recommendation? Stick with AAA or AA grades. You're in for the sure money, not the risk.

Either way, you need to make sure they're carefully vetted.

<u>How to invest in corporate bonds</u>: If you don't have the time or expertise to do this, use companies like Wint Wealth and GoldenPi to help you pick the right bond.

Corporate bond investing is like lending money to the suits in the corner office. You collect interest while they make the tough decisions.

2.2 Millionaires tell me real estate.

Bottom line:
Real estate investment = bragging rights at family parties.
It has its rewards. Can create passive income.
It has its downsides: it's illiquid, requires upfront capital, maintenance and time.
REITs offer a simpler entry. They let you tap into property perks without the heavy lifting.

Real estate in India isn't just property; it's a status update.
'Look, Ma, I bought a house!'

It's a great option to diversify your portfolio.
It's less volatile than stocks or bonds.
It's a good way to make some passive income.
You buy property, become a landlord (woohoo!) and enjoy your rental income.

The catch? You have to be able to afford it.

Real estate requires some serious upfront capital. If you opt for smaller plots, the rental income may not be lucrative.

Also, it isn't really liquid.
To access your money you have to go through the process of selling your property, which can take a lot of time.

REITs (real estate investment trusts) are yet another option.
They're cooler, less messy and cheaper!

REITs own and operate properties, make income from them.
They distribute rent among unit holders.
So, it's like buying a fraction of a property.
You buy units, becoming part owner of some swanky commercial space.
Think of it as mutual funds for real estate.

You can invest in a single unit of REIT and purchase units through a demat account, the same way you would buy shares in a listed company.

How to invest in REITs: If you don't have the time or expertise to do this, buy REITs from the stock market using platforms such as Zerodha (Kite), Groww, Angel One, Upstox, ICICI Securities, etc.

Real estate investing is like a relationship. At first, it's all about location, location, location. But after a while, it has to do with renovation, renovation, renovation.

2.3 Personal Finance creators say mutual funds.

> Bottom line:
> Mutual Funds = stock market's beginner-friendly zone.
> Let the experts manage, while you invest.

Mutual funds (MFs) let you pool your money with that of other investors to 'mutually' buy stocks, bonds and other assets.

They're run by professional fund managers.

MFs give you the flexibility to invest as specifically or generically as you want.

Invest in large companies only. Or mid-sized companies. Or small companies only. Or all.

Invest in the tech sector. Or in health care. Or in multiple sectors.

You get the flexibility to pick the broad themes you wish to invest in.

They allow fractional ownership—super cost-efficient.

You want to own multiple stocks.
But you can't afford them individually, at their minimum price.
You want to own stocks, bonds and other assets. You can't afford to buy those individually either.

Mutual funds to the rescue!
The MF buys these stocks or assets. You buy a unit of the MF.
Invest as low as ₹100, and you still get exposure to all the investments in the fund and the income they generate.

You get to rely on other people's expertise and experience, which you may not have.
You may not have the expertise to pick stocks.
Or know which sectors to bet on.
An expert does the research, takes care of the hard part.
A fund manager rebalances, updates the fund from time to time.

MFs charge a fee: the total expense ratio (TER) for their operating costs.

If you invest ₹50,000 at a 2% TER, you're paying ₹1000 to the fund.

The remaining ₹49,000 is invested.

There are 2 types of MF plans: direct and regular.

→ Regular plans: Bought via advisers or brokers. They get a commission, so these plans cost you more.

→ Direct plans: Bought straight from the mutual fund, typically on their website. Go for these—always!

There are 3 types of mutual funds.

→ Debt mutual funds

These funds invest in assets with a fixed rate of return.

Include corporate bonds, government bonds; could also include FDs.

Good if you want stable returns.

→ Equity or growth mutual funds
These funds invest in equity—that is, the stock market.
Higher risk than debt funds, potentially higher returns.

→ Hybrid or balanced mutual funds
Combination of debt and equity. The ratio of the 2 depends on your risk appetite.

A few things to note when investing in MFs:
→ Save on taxes where you can
Leverage Section 80C of the old tax regime to get exemptions up to ₹1.5 lakh on your yearly income.
ELSS (equity-linked savings scheme) is a popular tax saver.
These funds are spread across various market caps and come with a 3-year lock-in.

→ Check the historical returns of the fund
Review fund performance across different time periods.

Assess fund performance across market phases. But past success doesn't promise future results. You can look this up online, on sites like Moneycontrol.com or ETMoney.com.

→ Compare fund performance with a benchmark
For example, a large-cap fund can be compared with a broad-based benchmark index like NIFTY 50.
It should ideally do better than the benchmark. Yes, that was a no-brainer.

→ Look at the size of the fund or assets under management (AUM)
AUM simply means the total pooled in money from investors such as us.
I'd recommend funds with AUM of minimum ₹1000 crore.

→ Check the expense ratio
For index mutual funds, the expense ratio should not be more than 0.5%.
For others, 0.5–1% is acceptable.
Above 1.5% is considered high.

→ Check for exit load
This is a penalty you have to pay if you redeem early.
Ideally, there should be no exit load.
Exit load for 1 year is acceptable (you wouldn't want to sell before that as it is).
Above 1 year is considered high.

How to invest in mutual funds: Directly, through the asset management company, offline, or through their websites and apps. Or through platforms like . . . you know the drill! Zerodha (Coin), Groww, Angel One, Upstox, ICICI Securities, etc.

Mutual funds are the only place where you can have a diverse group of assets working for you, without the drama of office politics.

3. High Risk

3.1 Uncle says stock market trading.

> Bottom line:
> Trading requires deep insights, time and involvement.
> Not for beginners or busy peeps.
> Definitely not for the faint-hearted.

Investing and trading?
Often used interchangeably. Not the same thing.

Trading is, well . . . just that. Trading.
You buy. You sell.
You're in today, out today!
Traders watch the short-term price changes of stocks.
Bet on market rises and dips. Try to make money on short-term price movements.
It's about timing. It's about trends.
Buy low. Sell high.

Aim to maximize returns daily, monthly or quarterly.

It's a high-risk trading game for high returns.

Investing in the stock market is quite different.

You buy the shares of a company (or several companies) that you believe will grow.

You now own the stocks (also called 'delivery').

You own part of the company.

As a shareholder, you're invested in the company and its growth.

How to trade in stocks: Trade in stocks from brokerages like Zerodha (Kite), Groww, Angel One, Upstox, ICICI Securities, etc.

Stock trading is like a Balaji soap opera. There's drama, excitement, betrayal and frequent heartbreaks, but you can't resist tuning in every day.

3.2 Tech bros tell me crypto.

> Bottom line:
> Invest in a cryptocurrency if you believe in its long-term prospects.
> Be willing to absorb large price swings and potential losses.

Crypto's buzzing, and not just on X.

Its allure is undeniable.
It is challenging traditional finance.
It is the maverick questioning the norm.
Plus, the dream of big wins!

Like with everything speculative, this hope is addictive.
But here's the thing with crypto: it's also risky.
Prices swing, and they swing big.
You can check it 5 times a day, and the prices can vary wildly.
One day you see a 10% jump; the next day, it might plummet just as much. Even big players

like Bitcoin and Ethereum have ridden this roller coaster.

Cryptocurrencies can be launched by anyone! That's their beauty. That's also their danger.
Lack of regulation means no safety nets in case of scams or big losses.
Personally, I lean towards the relatively stabler coins—Bitcoin, Ethereum and Solana.
But do your own research before diving into any crypto investment.

Invest only if you're willing to play the long game (like with all other investments).
Be ready to absorb large price swings.
There's no room for knee-jerk reactions here.
FOMO buys and panic sells? Bad strategies. Always.

ALWAYS keep this asset class to 5% or less of your portfolio.

<u>How to invest in crypto</u>: Look at options like WazirX, CoinSwitch or Binance to buy crypto.

Investing in crypto is like having a pet rock that can fetch a Lamborghini one day and then turn into a paperweight the next.

So Many Assets? I Am Confused.

Everyone's confused, don't you worry.
Here is a good rule to start with:

⇒ Consider the 100x rule for asset allocation.
Subtract your age (x) from 100.
The result is the percentage you should ideally invest in equity.

Say you're 25.
(100) – (25) = Invest 75% in equities.
The other 25%? Put it in low-risk assets like sovereign gold bonds or EPF/PPF.

However, this rule is too generic and will not always work.
I share a more detailed approach, based on your age and income, in the chapter titled 'And Manage My Money Well'.

Exception to the rule: Don't invest money you need in the short term into equity or hard-to-sell assets.

For instance, if you need money for a course in 6–8 months, keep that money in liquid assets.

⇒ Pick your assets as per your risk profile and the returns you're looking for.
Younger people typically have a long-term horizon and can afford to take some risk.
It's a personal decision, though! You need to gauge your comfort with risk—and the accompanying returns.

→ Use the 'Rule of 72' to understand how long it'll take to double your investment.
The rule states:
72 / rate of return of your investment = approximate number of years taken to double your money

If your portfolio gives you:
- 12% returns, expect your money to double in ~6 years (72/12).
- 15% returns, expect your money to double in ~4.8 years (72/15).

- 18% returns, expect your money to double in ~4 years (72/18).

Use this rule for individual assets too.
E.g., if you invest in an FD with ~6% rate of return, your money will double in 12 years.
If you invest in a mutual fund with 10% return, your money will double in 7.2 years.
If you invest in crypto with no typical rate of return, you don't know when it will double.
It may double tomorrow or go to 0.

⇒ Diversify. Then double down on what is working.
Spread your bets.
Not just one asset.
Love gold? We all do. Still doesn't mean we put everything there.
Partial to tech? Nice, but spread beyond it.
Work in health care? Super, but you alone can't influence the outcome of the whole sector (unfortunately).
Diversify within assets, too.

Once you're in it and only when you understand it, double down on what is working.
Overdiversification may not yield supernormal returns.
Owning more of what is working may.

⇒ Remember, you're playing for the long term.

If the market goes up and down, does this mean you do not invest?
NO! It means you need to have a long-term horizon to investing.

You can either think of investing as a quick fling.
You're in when it's good.
You're out when it's bad.

Or you can think of it as a committed relationship.
You give it time. Ride out the cycles.
Stick with it through the highs and lows.

Difference between Tinder and Shaadi.com, perhaps?

Whether you're a free spirit or all about commitment, with finances, play the long game.

Crucial reminder:
The most important cost in investing to watch out for is the psychological one.

No investment is worth it if it gives you returns while taking away your sleep.
On the other hand, no investment is worth it if it just sleeps, while you do all the work.

How to Begin Investing: The Mechanics of It All

Investing is a good thing. We all (hopefully) get this!

Starting off can be pretty confusing though.

First, the basics.

→ Save. Invest. Repeat.

The 50:30:20 budgeting rule is a good place to start.

-   50% of your monthly income for your needs (EMI/rent, food, utilities, bills).
-   30% for wants (phone, car, gadgets, vacay).
-   20% straight to investments.

→ Build your safety net.

Build your emergency fund.

Invest in health insurance and life insurance.

→ Save ALL possible taxes.

You can (and should) invest in assets that cut your taxable income.

ELSS, EPF, PPF, NPS, your insurance premiums—all fall under 80C deductions up to ₹1.5 lakh per year.
Make these investments!

Open a demat account to start investing in equity.
A demat account works like an electronic bank for investments: stocks, mutual funds, bonds, ETFs.
E.g., if you buy company shares, it's entered in electronic form in your demat account.

It's mandatory to have a demat account for equity investing.
Choose from platforms like Zerodha, Groww, 5Paisa, Upstox, etc., to open your demat account—plenty of options to choose from!
You'll need a PAN card and an Aadhaar card to get started, along with a few other documents that serve as your ID proof and address proof, and carry your bank details.

SIPs: Invest regularly to smooth out market volatility.

Systematic investment plans (SIPs) are not schemes or investment products in themselves.

Think of them as EMIs.

Just that instead of paying a bank, you are paying yourself.

Sweet!

- An SIP is a financial ritual.

Every month, on a set date, money auto-transfers from your account to a chosen mutual fund.

Makes saving feel less heavy on the wallet.

- SIPs are great to manage market mood swings.

With SIPs, you buy at regular, set intervals, at different market prices.

You get more units when prices dip, and less when they peak.

This averages out your investment cost.

It's your shield against market mood swings.

-    They harness the power of compounding.
With SIPs, you stay consistent.
It's not just that your main amount grows.
The returns on that amount grow, too.
Over time, this multiplies your money.

-    Pick direct over regular plans.
Direct plans generally have a lower expense ratio.
This translates to higher returns in the long run.
If you're already in a regular plan, though, and want to switch to direct, check for potential exit loads and capital gain tax implications.

-    Pick your platform.
Numerous platforms exist—Coin, Groww, ICICI Securities, Angel Broking, Upstox.
Each comes with unique features and offerings.
Research and pick a platform that aligns with your investment goals and comfort.

-    Don't stop mutual fund SIPs.
'Market is low', 'returns are not good'.
No excuses. Don't stop.

Start!
Personal finance is personal for a reason.
Your approach is yours. Own it.
Never let anyone push you to invest in something that makes you uncomfortable.
Never invest in anything with the belief that you can't lose.

Sometimes, you will be luckier than others. Other times, you won't.
Sometimes, you will outsmart others. Other times, you won't.

Your only persistent edge in investing is:
- Starting earlier than others.
- Being consistent.
- Being more patient than others.

'The problem is that no one wants to get rich slowly.'

—Warren Buffett

Think about This

-   Start investing as early as you can. Even if it's a small amount. Compound interest multiplies your money at an accelerated rate—you earn interest on your interest. The longer your money stays invested, the better for you.

-   Your risk tolerance determines how you invest.
    Assets with lower risk typically give you lower returns.
    Assets with higher risk could give you higher returns but also higher losses.
    The wise ones balance risk.

-   How to balance risk?
-   Asset allocation.

Invest across different assets with different risks.

- Good rule to manage risk?
- 100x rule: if x is your age, then invest x% in fixed income (lower risk) and 100x% in equities (higher risk).

- Use the Rule of 72 to understand how long it will take to double your investment.
The rule states: *72/rate of return of your investment = approximate no. of years taken to double your money.*

- Remember: You're playing for the long term!

Do This

- Open a demat account to start investing in equity.

  Pick a reliable brokerage or bank to open a demat account and dive into equity investments.

  You can do this online, through platforms such as Zerodha, Groww, 5Paisa or Upstox.

- Decide your asset-allocation strategy.
  - Decide how much you will invest in equity (the 100x rule is a good start).
  - Within equity, decide how much risk you're willing to take.
    - How much in large-cap mutual funds?
    - How much in mid-cap mutual funds?

- How much in small-cap mutual funds?
- Within fixed income/safer assets, decide how you will split it among different assets (e.g., EPF, NPS, bonds, gold, etc.).

- Automate your investments.
Create a separate account to park your savings (to invest!).
Set up auto-transfers from your salary account to your investment accounts.

- Start systematic investment plans (SIPs)—they're great to balance out market volatility.

AND MANAGE MY MONEY WELL

'Most people overestimate what they can do in a year, and they massively underestimate what they can accomplish in a decade or two. The fact is: you are not a manager of circumstance, you're the architect of your life's experience.'

—Tony Robbins

The job I got after graduating post my MBA from the Indian School of Business paid me a lot of money.
So I spent it to show that I had a lot of money.
Bought a car.
Upgraded the house.
Bought appliances.
Got a credit card.

In my 20s, I had a 'rich mindset'.
All about spending.
All about flexing.
Living for the present.

Now, at 40, I wish I had the 'wealthy mindset'.
Planned for the future, while still living life.
Built and grown wealth consistently.
For financial security.
For financial independence.

Our Money Decisions Today Determine the Quality of Our Lives Tomorrow

Money provides us with opportunities.

It drives our ambitions.

It fuels our dreams.

It gives us freedom.

It gives us comfort.

Money isn't just currency. It's a lifeline.

But here's what's strange:

For something so crucial, we don't have a game plan.

Most of us are just going with the flow.

Winging it as we go along.

In our 20s, we're all about the carefree life.

'My life, my rules' and all that.

Then, the 30s come around.

Adulting crashes the party with bills and grown-up stuff.

We hit the 40s. 50s. Retirement isn't too far off.

Kids start talking about college fees.

You need a new laptop. The kids want one too.
We don't feel as healthy as we used to.
But we're making those ends meet. Hanging in there.

Still . . . there's a nagging feeling.
We wish we had planned better.

The older we get, the more money matters.
But in our 20s, we don't see that.
We miss out on the game-changing potential of investing.
We miss out on the magic of compounding.
We miss out on giving our money enough time to grow.

Starting early is the way to go. But it's never too late to start.
Get intentional about your money.
It's your money story—YOU write it!

Your Financial Plan Must Evolve with Each Life Stage

Picture this:

You're in your 20s, earning ₹5 lakh annually.

You're living with your parents, few bills, no dependents.

Life's great!

Jump to your 30s: that same ₹5 lakh feels tighter.

Family responsibilities grow, health concerns arise, your parents are also getting old.

Now, in your 40s, that ₹5 lakh could spell disaster.

Retirement is getting closer. What's the plan, bro?

This situation may be unlikely, but the point of this example is still valid.

Your money game HAS to level up with increasing age and income.

So, let's visualize your life across 3 decades—
20s, 30s and 40s.
And across 3 income bands—annual salary of
less than ₹3 lakh, ₹3–9 lakh and above ₹9 lakh.

There you have it! A 3x3 grid. Nine different
combos. Nine game plans.
Find your place in the grid.
Think of this as the only 3x3 cheat sheet you
need for the game of life.

Financial Planning by Age and Salary

Age	Your 20s
Income	<₹3 lakh per annum

Headline: You have time. Take risks. Find ways to boost your income.

- First, financial protection.
  Emergency fund: Build for 3 months.
  Health insurance: For your parents. They need it. You can be without one right now.
  Life insurance: Can wait till your 30s. Or till your income exceeds ₹9 lakh annually.

- Don't spend more than 20% on your desires. At this income you can't afford to spend more than 20% of your monthly salary (after tax, my friend!) on things you desire.

- Find ways to increase your income.
  Upskilling is a great way to do this.
  Study further, start (and complete) online courses.

Take up odd jobs, earn more money.
Look for other active or passive income opportunities.
Read about this in detail in the chapter titled 'Now, I Really Want to Earn Some Money!'.

- Invest at least 30% of your income!

TIME is your biggest, biggest asset. That's what you're going to leverage.

Most of your portfolio should go into the stock market.

To maximize the power of compounding and get yourself higher returns!

A small portion will go into fixed-return assets (for safety).

It will provide you with a steady interest.

Skip assets like gold, real estate and crypto till you increase your income.

Here's a potential investment plan (for the amount you invest):

- *25% to fixed-return assets (FD/EPF/PPF/ debt mutual funds)*

- *75% to mutual funds*

Within that:

- 40% in NIFTY 50 mutual funds SIP
- 30% in mid-cap mutual funds SIP
- 30% in small-cap mutual funds SIP

- AVOID credit cards and loans.

They'll just invite overspending, which you can't handle at this income level.

Age	Your 20s
Income	Between ₹3–9 lakh per annum

Headline: You have time. Take risks.
Live large, but keep that spending in check.

- First, financial protection.
  Emergency fund: Build for 6 months.
  Health insurance: For yourself and your parents (can be combined, if you are single).
  Life insurance: Get life insurance coverage at 20x your salary, with the ability to increase it later.

- Don't spend more than 25% on your desires.
  You're young. A steady income is rolling in.
  It's easy to get carried away.
  Don't be.
  Stay within 25% of your monthly after-tax earnings.
  Before you spend, ask yourself: Do I really want it?

- You have time. Use it to grow your investments.
  The stock market will be your best friend.
  To maximize the power of compounding and get yourself higher returns!
  Go big on small-cap and mid-cap mutual funds.
  Risky? Sure, but you can afford the risk.
  Time is your cushion.
  Think of them as calculated risks!

Balance it out with stable fixed-return investments.
With a fixed interest, they provide a safety net.

- Diversify: try gold, real estate/REITs, crypto.
  Real estate needs a hefty upfront sum.
  REITs? Just ₹500 and you're in.
  Crypto's volatile. Pick it up ONLY if you understand it and if you believe in its long-term potential.
  Not because others are doing it.

Here's a potential investment plan (for the amount you invest):

- *20% in fixed-return assets (FD/EPF/PPF/ debt mutual funds)*

- *75% in mutual funds*
  Within that
  - 30% in NIFTY 50 mutual funds SIP
  - 40% in mid-cap mutual funds SIP
  - 30% in small-cap mutual funds SIP

- *5% to gold; or 5% to real estate/REITs; or 5% to crypto*

- A credit card is okay.
  Do not get one with an annual fee. Get a free one.
  If it's hard to get, consider an FD-backed one. It uses the money in your FD to give you a credit limit.
  A credit card helps build a good credit score. Don't forget to pay your bills in full and on time, though!

- A loan is okay. But ONLY for education or a car.

  Education can be an investment in your future.

  Hopefully leading to better jobs and income.

  A car can save on commuting costs.

  Plus, acing your loans builds a solid credit history.

  ONLY take on what you can pay back easily.

  Definitely NO personal loans!

Age	Your 20s
Income	Above ₹9 lakh per annum

Headline: You have time AND money. Live your best life, and keep investing smartly!

- First, financial protection.
  Emergency fund: Build for 12 months.
  Health insurance: For yourself and your parents (combined, with top-up).
  Life insurance: Get life insurance coverage at 25x your salary, with the ability to increase it later.

- Don't spend more than 30% on your desires. You're young and restless.
  Income's looking good too: you deserve your own 'fun fund'.
  Keep a generous 30% to splurge: you've earned it.
  But remember, it's easy to overspend when things are good.

- Invest consistently—leverage time.
  Focus more on the stock market for growth.
  Go big on small-cap and mid-cap MFs for risky but big gains over the long term.

  Balance the risk with steady returns from fixed investments.
  Keep only a small chunk here, though!
  Fixed returns barely keep up with inflation.

- Diversify those investments: try gold, real estate/REITs, crypto.
  Real estate needs more upfront money.
  REITs: start small, with ₹500.
  Crypto's volatile and complex—invest only if you understand it.
  This mix aims for higher returns while keeping things in check.

  Here's a potential investment plan (for the amount you invest):
- *15% in fixed-return assets (FD/EPF/PPF/debt mutual funds)*

- *80% in mutual funds*
  Within that
  - 25% in NIFTY 50 mutual funds SIP
  - 40% in mid-cap mutual funds SIP
  - 35% in small-cap mutual funds SIP

- *5% to gold; or 5% to real estate or REITs; or 5% to crypto*

- Get a credit card. Make it work for you.
  It's great for building a good credit score.
  Plus reward points and freebies. Why say no, at this income?
  Don't forget to pay your (full) bill every month!
  Read about this in detail in the chapter titled 'So That I Can Spend It (Wisely)'.

- A loan is fine. But ONLY for education or a car.
  No home loan as yet, even though you can afford it.
  Because you're way too young to commit.

Age	Your 30s
Income	<₹3 lakh per annum

Headline: Protect your savings. Focus on income growth.

- First, financial protection.
  Emergency fund: Build for 6 months. At this age, you need protection.
  Health insurance: For your parents. At this age, they need it, more than you do.
  Life insurance: Get coverage at 15x your salary.

- Don't spend more than 15% on your desires.
  You have no choice, my friend.
  Your income is limited.
  So your desires need to reduce too.

- Find ways to increase your income.
  Don't just stick to your day job for income—think beyond!

There's a bunch of ways to earn actively or passively.
Take your skills and talents to the next level by freelancing or consulting.
Beef up skills with online courses.
Read about this in detail in the chapter titled 'Now, I Really Want to Earn Some Money!'.

- Invest while playing safe.
  In your 30s, time is still on your side, but it's more precious than before.
  Let's use it strategically.

  Focus the core of your investing on the stock market.
  Let compounding work its magic.
  Keep a large share in fixed assets.
  They offer stability and lower portfolio risk.
  Give assets like gold, real estate and crypto a miss.
  We don't have the income for that right now.

Here's a potential investment plan (for the amount you invest):

- *30% goes in fixed-return assets (FD/EPF/ PPF/debt mutual funds)*

- *70% goes in mutual funds*
  Within that
  - 70% in NIFTY 50 mutual funds SIP
  - 25% in mid-cap mutual funds SIP
  - 5% in small-cap mutual funds SIP

- AVOID credit cards and loans.
  They invite overspending.
  Juggling debt on a tight income can be tough.

Age	Your 30s
Income	Between ₹3–9 lakh per annum

Headline: Decent place to be. Time is (still) your best asset.
Don't be greedy. Don't be scared. Stick to the plan!

- First, financial protection.
  Emergency fund: Build for 9 months. Since you can afford to.
  Health insurance: For yourself + spouse + kids and for your parents (with top-up).
  Life insurance: Get coverage at 20x your salary, with the ability to increase it later.

- Don't spend more than 20% on your desires. Think of it as your 'personal indulgence budget' (on after-tax income).
  But don't cross that line.
  This range lets you treat yourself and invest smartly. It's a happy middle ground.

- Don't make hasty investment decisions.
  Don't let shortcuts and quick gains tempt you.
  They can cloud your financial judgement.
  Push you to take bigger risks than necessary.
  Say no to spur-of-the-moment choices driven by emotions.
  Stick to your investment plan even during market volatility.

- Find ways to increase your income instead.
  Choose side gigs that align with your passions and skills.
  Think freelancing, consulting and more.
  Read about this in detail in the chapter titled 'Now, I Really Want to Earn Some Money!'.

- Make your money work for you.
  In your 30s, seeking stability makes sense.
  But remember, time is your ally. Use it to leverage compounding!
  Dedicate a smaller portion to fixed-return assets.

They keep things steady and dial down overall risk.
But their returns might not outpace inflation by much.

The core of your portfolio should focus on the stock market.
For growth and higher returns.
NIFTY 50 takes the lead, with consistent earnings.
A little less goes into the riskier mid-cap and small-cap options.
Avoid assets like gold, real estate and crypto.
Consider them once your income rises.

Here's a potential investment plan (for the amount you invest):
- *25% goes in fixed-return assets (FD/EPF/ PPF/debt mutual funds)*

- *75% goes in mutual funds*
  - *Within that*
  - 60% in NIFTY 50 mutual funds SIP

- 30% in mid-cap mutual funds SIP
- 10% in small-cap mutual funds SIP

- A credit card is okay at this stage.
  Pay the bill in full. ALWAYS.
  This allows you to build a credit score without taking a loan.

- Please avoid loans.
  Let your income grow before considering loans.
  No home, not yet.
  A car, only if you really need it.

Age	Your 30s
Income	Above ₹9 lakh per annum

Headline: A good place to be.
Be consistent and smart with your investments.

- First, financial protection.
  Emergency fund: Build for 12 months.
  Health insurance: For yourself + spouse + kids and for your parents (with top-up).
  Life insurance: Get coverage at 25x your salary.

- Don't spend more than 30% on your desires.
  Your solid income sets a strong foundation. So, you get to spend 30% after-tax income on your desires. Yay!

- Focus on passive income sources.
  Your talents and skills can fetch you passive income.

Think freelancing, consulting and more.
Anything you wanted to pursue but didn't have the financial means to.
With your stable income, this could be a good way to explore your passion.
Read about this in detail in the chapter titled 'Now, I Really Want to Earn Some Money!'.

- Invest consistently.
  Investing regularly can be a game changer.
  You've got the advantage of time AND money.
  Let compounding work its magic over the years.
  It's not about timing the market.
  It's about giving your investments time to grow.

Here's a potential investment plan (for the amount you invest):
- *20% goes in fixed-return assets (FD/EPF/ PPF/debt mutual funds)*

- *75% goes in mutual funds*
  Within that
  - 50% in NIFTY 50 mutual funds SIP
  - 35% in mid-cap mutual funds SIP
  - 15% in small-cap mutual funds SIP

- *5% goes to gold or real estate or REITs.*

- Get a credit card.
  At this income, benefit from the 30–45 day interest-free loan.
  The chance to build your credit score and enjoy freebies.
  You've earned it!
  Read about this in detail in the chapter titled 'So That I Can Spend It (Wisely)'.

- A loan is okay as long as it's for a home or a car.
  Think of them as good ways to enjoy your money.
  But always be in a hurry to pay off the loan.

Remember, 1 extra EMI per year + 10% higher EMI every year reduces a 25-year loan to just 10 years!

Read about this in detail in the chapter titled 'So That I Can Spend It (Wisely)'.

Age	Your 40s
Income	<₹3 lakh per annum

Headline: A dangerous place to be. Protect. Focus on growing income.

- First, financial protection.
  Emergency fund: Build for 9 months. DO NOT think of anything else before this.
  Health insurance: For yourself + spouse + kids and for your parents. CRITICAL!
  Life insurance: Get coverage at 10x your salary. CRITICAL at this stage.

- Can't spend more than 10% on your desires.
  You have wants. So does your family.
  But remember, your income has its limits.
  So, adjust your desires accordingly.
  The key is to live within your means.

- Don't fall for get-rich-quick schemes.
  When money's tight, get-rich-quick schemes can be tempting.

Sure, they dangle the idea of quick cash. But they come with sneaky risks.
And watch out—some are just scams.
The potential loss might outstrip any gains.
In your 40s, wiping out your savings isn't the route to take.

- Find ways to increase your income.
  Put your skills to work. Find odd jobs to supplement your income.
  Hunt for higher-paying roles.
  Read about this in detail in the chapter titled 'Now, I Really Want to Earn Some Money!'.

- Play it safe. Invest regularly, but very cautiously.
  Let's steer clear of any crazy risks.
  The smart investment play is balance: split it 50-50.
  Half for steady, fixed returns. Half for the stock market.

In the stock market, 80% hangs with the reliable NIFTY 50.

20% in mid-cap MFs for more growth.

Small-cap MFs? Not at this time—they are too risky for your age.
Gold, real estate and crypto? Nope, not enough income to digest these yet.

Here's a potential investment plan (for the amount you invest):
- *50% goes in fixed-return assets (FD/EPF/ PPF/debt mutual funds)*

- *50% goes in mutual funds*
  Within that
    - 80% in NIFTY 50 mutual funds SIP
    - 20% in mid-cap mutual funds SIP
    - 0% in small-cap mutual funds SIP

- ABSOLUTELY NO credit cards and loans. With lower earnings, repayments can be a hassle.

Age	Your 40s
Income	Between ₹3–9 lakh per annum

Headline: A tricky place to be.
Focus on side income. Choose renting over buying.

- First, financial protection.
  Emergency fund: Build for 9 months.
  Health insurance: For yourself + spouse + kids and for your parents.
  Life insurance: Get coverage at 15x your salary.

- No more than 15% on your desires.
  At this stage, you've got big responsibilities.
  Maybe a home loan already, kids' education, retirement planning—prioritize these.
  By keeping wants to 15%, you keep a good chunk for needs. And leave some for investments.
  This keeps debt and stress at bay.

- Consider renting a house over buying.

  Wanting a home in your 40s is understandable.

  But with limited income, renting is a wiser choice.

  You don't want more money going out—loan interest, taxes, maintenance of your home.

  Renting lets you save for different things—investments, assets.

  Avoids tying up a big part of your funds.

  Gives you flexibility for other opportunities.

  Read about this in detail in the chapter titled 'So That I Can Spend It (Wisely)'.

- Find ways to increase your income.

  Put your expertise to work. Try consulting, freelancing or side gigs.

  Focus on upskilling to get higher-paying roles.

  Reach out to your connections for job referrals, new opportunities.

  Read about this in detail in the chapter titled 'Now, I Really Want to Earn Some Money!'.

- Continue investing. YES, even at this age! In your 40s, your responsibilities take centre stage.
  Avoid the extremes—no ultra-safe or super-risky moves.
  With a steady income, try a 40–60 split.

  40% in steady fixed returns, the rest in the stock market.
  Fixed returns suit your age and income. The stable anchor in your portfolio.
  In the variable realm, it's 75% in NIFTY 50 for dependability.
  Add 25% in mid-cap MFs for extra gains.

  Small-cap MFs, real estate and crypto? I'd suggest you skip them—too risky.

Here's a potential investment plan (for the amount you invest):
- *40% goes in fixed-return assets (FD/EPF/ PPF/debt mutual funds)*

- *60% goes in mutual funds*
  Within that
    - 75% in NIFTY 50 mutual funds SIP
    - 25% in mid-cap mutual funds SIP
    - 0% in small-cap mutual funds SIP

- Avoid credit cards and loans.
  These can lead to unnecessary debt and financial stress.
  Neither of which you need right now.

Age	Your 40s
Income	Above ₹9 lakh per annum

Headline: A safe place to be.
Protect yourself. Invest consistently.

- First, financial protection.
  Emergency fund: Build for 12 months.
  Health insurance: For yourself + spouse + kids and for your parents (with top-up).
  Life insurance: Get coverage at 20x–25x your salary.

- Don't spend more than 25–30% on your desires.
  When you're in a good financial space, splurging can be tempting.
  But don't forget the golden 25% rule—buy only stuff you really want.
  Otherwise, you'll end up with things you will regret having bought. And with less money!
  Keep the focus on needs, protection and future goals.

- Focus on consistent investing.
  You are NOT late.
  Start investing, if you haven't already.
  You still have time.
  You certainly have money.
  Make that money work for you.

  Your investment strategy:
  Let's take some calculated risks with your strong income.
  Around 30% in fixed returns. The rest in the stock market.

  Fixed returns maintain stability.
  Among the variables, 70% goes to the more stable NIFTY 50.
  Allocate 30% to mid-cap mutual funds for that growth push.
  But for now, small-cap MFs take a back seat—a tad too risky.
  No real estate and crypto either.

Here's a potential investment plan (for the amount you invest):

- *30% goes in fixed-return assets (FD/EPF/PPF/debt mutual funds)*

- *70% goes in mutual funds*
  Within that
  - 70% in NIFTY 50 mutual funds SIP
  - 30% in mid-cap mutual funds SIP
  - 0% in small-cap mutual funds SIP

- Get a credit card.
  Use it wisely (within your limits).
  Pay the bill in full and on time.
  Enjoy the freebies.
  Build that credit score!
  Read about this in detail in the chapter titled 'So That I Can Spend It (Wisely)'.

- A home loan at this stage Is okuy.
  It's a chance to invest in a valuable asset—your own home.
  And get tax benefits!

As retirement nears, it also offers stability. With a solid income, managing repayments is also easier.

In the End . . .

Your financial path is shaped by your age and your income.

Along with what you want in life and your responsibilities.

You have the cheat sheet, but you're holding the cards.

Only YOU decide how to play them.

'You can do it like it's a great weight on you, or you can do it like it's a part of the dance.'

—Ram Dass

Do This!

Find out where you are on this grid. Make adjustments to your financial plan accordingly.

- Emergency fund/health insurance/ life insurance
- Max amount for wants
- How much to invest in fixed-return assets
- How much to invest in mutual funds
  - ○ Large cap
  - ○ Mid cap
  - ○ Small cap
- Gold/real estate/other assets
- Credit cards/loans
- Loans
- Figure out where you will be on the grid 5 years from now and how you will have to adjust your financial plan accordingly.

Your 20s

Income			
	Below ₹3 lakh	**Between ₹3–9 lakh**	**Above ₹9 lakh**
Emergency fund	3 months	6 months	12 months
Health insurance	For parents	For yourself + parents	For yourself + parents
Life insurance	In your 30s Or income >₹9 lakh	20x of salary	25x of salary
Max wants	20%	25%	30%
Fixed-return assets	25%	20%	15%
Equity investments	75%	75%	80%
NIFTY 50 MF	40%	30%	25%
Mid-cap MF	30%	40%	40%
Small-cap MF	30%	30%	35%
Gold/real estate/others	No	5%	5%
Credit cards	No	FD-backed	FD-backed
Loans	No	Only for education or a car	Only for education or a car

Your 30s

	Income		
	Below ₹3 lakh	**Between ₹3–9 lakh**	**Above ₹9 lakh**
Emergency fund	6 months	9 months	12 months
Health insurance	For yourself + spouse + kids For your parents	For yourself + spouse + kids For your parents	For yourself + spouse + kids For your parents
Life insurance	15x of salary	20x of salary	25x of salary
Max wants	15%	20%	30%
Fixed-return assets	30%	25%	20%
Equity investments	70%	75%	75%
NIFTY 50 MF	70%	60%	50%
Mid-cap MF	25%	30%	35%
Small-cap MF	5%	10%	15%
Gold/real estate/others	No	No	5%
Credit cards	No	FD-backed credit card	FD-backed credit card
Loans	No	No	ONLY for home or a car

Your 40s

Income		
	Below ₹3 lakh	**Between ₹3–9 lakh**	**Above ₹9 lakh**
Emergency fund	9 months	9 months	12 months
Health insurance	For yourself + spouse + kids For your parents	For yourself + spouse + kids For your parents	For yourself For your parents
Life insurance	15x of salary	20x of salary	25x of salary
Max wants	10%	15%	25%
Fixed-return assets	50%	40%	30%
Equity investments	50%	60%	70%
NIFTY 50 MF	80%	75%	70%
Mid-cap MF	20%	25%	30%
Small-cap MF	0%	0%	0%
Gold/real estate/others	No	No	No
Credit cards	No	No	FD-backed credit card
Loans	No	No	ONLY for a home

I KNOW I'LL
MAKE MISTAKES

'Nothing in life is to be feared.
It's only to be understood.'

—Marie Curie

When I first spoke in public, I was clueless.
I froze. No words came out.
When I made my first investment, I was clueless.
Crossed my fingers, hoping for the best.
When I made my first Instagram post, I was clueless.
Got 3 likes. Not a single comment.

Everyone starts at zero.

You will make mistakes. In fact, the system wants you to make mistakes.
Start, anyway!

Circumvent the system by learning from your own mistakes.
Beat the system by learning from the mistakes of others.

Mistake #1: Believing the 'Zero-Risk' Lie

Everything in life carries a risk.
Dating. Work. Career.
And yes, money.

Some risks are obvious. Right in front of us.
Gambling. Investing in crypto or NFTs.
Confessing that you like pineapple on pizza.
Telling your mom the actual price of the gift you
got her.

But just because something is risky, doesn't
mean it should not be or cannot be done.

Risk can't be eliminated.
It can only be understood and managed.

When you're young, your ability to take risks is
higher.
Not because you've got it all figured out.
Because you have time.
Time to recover from any damage that may be
caused by the risk.

Two independent truths exist when it comes to risk and money:

1. Low risk will almost always mean low returns. Or else everyone would be doing it.
   Takeaway: Your money will not grow in low-risk assets.

2. High risk need not always mean high returns. Or it wouldn't be called high risk after all.
   Takeaway: You won't get rich overnight just because you took a massive risk.

This is what I would do:
I'd play the long-term game, to manage (not eliminate) higher risk.

Here's an example:

The Possibilities
Future Returns and Nifty 50

Time (Years)	Worst Returns	Average Returns	Probability of	
			Negative Returns	Above 8%
1	-20%	13	25%	50%
3	-2%	13	15%	75%
5	5%	12	0	90%
10	6%	12	0	100%

SOURCE: JRL Money

Image copyright BCCL

If you invest in NIFTY 50 for a year, there's a 25% chance that you'll lose money.
Only a 50% chance that you'll beat inflation (8% returns pre tax).

If you invested in the same index for 5 years, there is ZERO chance (based on past data) that you will lose money.
And a 90% chance you will earn above 8%.

If you invest for 10 years, the chance of earning above 8% goes to nearly 100%!

Did you eliminate the risk? Nope.
You managed it, through time. Smart!

Mistake #2: Short-Term Thinking

YOLO is a drug. It intoxicates us.
Makes us believe that all money earned should
be spent.

'Live for today. You only live once!'

No—you don't live only once.
You live every day.
And you are going to live for a long time.

During this long time, there will come a phase
when your income will stop.
You will want to make a big purchase (or 10), for
which you will need a lot of money.
You will have an emergency situation (or 5),
where you will need a lot of money.

The need for instant gratification.
It's costlier than you think.

Live well, today.
Also, live responsibly.
Budget.

Max 30% of your income for your desires.
Minimum 20% for your future.

Keep that YOLO meter on. Monitor it.
Do it for yourself, and for those who'll walk beside you.

Mistake #3: Ignoring Inflation

Inflation isn't some abstract concept you read in books.

It's real.

Picture this:

You've saved ₹1 lakh. Awesome!

You keep it snug under your mattress.

A year goes by. You still have ₹1 lakh under that trusty mattress.

Yay! That's awesome, no?

No!

It can't buy the same amount of stuff as it could last year, though.

That phone or that vacation? They've become pricier.

Blame it on inflation. The silent money-eater.

It erodes your money's purchasing power. Bit by bit.

Think 5% inflation yearly.

Your ₹1 lakh is just ₹95,000 after 1 year in terms of buying power.

After 2 years? Closer to ₹91,000.
Like a slow leak.

Ten years go by.
Without smart investing, your money feels more like ₹50,000. Ouch!

When weighing your investment returns, don't just look at the absolute number.
Factor in inflation.
If your investment earns 5% and inflation is 5%, your real return is 0.
Inflation is real. And it's relentless.

Then there's that thing about reported inflation and YOUR personal inflation (aka lifestyle inflation).
The 5% that the government announces—it's quite possible that your expenses are growing faster than that every year.
That's because you're not the 'average' spender.
You spend on things not everyone spends on.

Your unique spending patterns—like frequent dining out, latest fashion buys, entertainment and travels—are different from others.

For many, the real inflation rate may hover closer to 8–9%.
Which means, if you want your money to grow, you have to earn AT LEAST 8% post tax every year.

Did I mention inflation is real? And it's relentless.

Mistake #4: Ignoring Taxes

Everyone thinks that taxes are a bummer.
Something we want to avoid. Painful. Ugh!
Flip the script:
They're badges of adulting success.
A statement of your financial well-being.
You're making money, so you're paying taxes.
It's proof of your work.

Scan this code for a complete guide to tax planning for salaried peeps.

Scan this code for tax tips for freelancers.

→ Capital gains tax
Capital gain = the profit you make when you sell an equity asset (stocks, mutual funds, ETFs) for higher than its purchase price.

Capital gains tax kicks in only when you sell.
E.g.: You bought stock for ₹500. Its value is now ₹600.

On paper, your profit is ₹100.
You don't pay tax on this. It's an unrealized gain.
ONLY when you sell this stock you make a profit
of ₹100.
That's realized gain.
You pay tax on only realized gain.

Types of taxes on realized capital gains:
- Short-term capital gain (STCG) tax
  <u>Duration</u>: If the asset is bought and sold within one year.
  <u>Tax</u>: 15% on the profit.
- Long-term capital gain (LTCG) tax
  <u>Duration</u>: If the asset is sold after a year of buying it.

Tax: 10% tax if your profit is >₹1 lakh.
If your profit is <₹1 lakh, no tax!

Finally: Taxes are a real thing.
Research, save where you can.
File your returns every year.
Or get an accountant to do it for you.

Mistake #5: Living beyond Your Means

Swipe. Click. Buy. Repeat.

New gadgets? Got it.

Super-cool shoes, sorry sneakers? Bought.

Ordering in every night? Why not?

Eating out every weekend? Absolutely!

Thanks to credit cards and easy-to-get EMIs, we think we have more money than we actually have.

We earn 1 rupee but spend 2.

Then we want to earn back the money we have lost.

So we make more mistakes. Fall for get-rich-quick schemes. Gamble.

DO NOT spend money that you DO NOT HAVE!

Mistake #6: Ego!

Ego is like your social media filter.
The 'Insta you' vs the raw, unfiltered you.

We spend our lives trying to keep our ego happy.
What will they think of me?
How can I shine brighter?
What can I buy that others will want?

Take a moment. Track your expenses for a week. Just 1 week.
How much of it truly sparks joy?
And how much is for others?

If it's for the world, it's your ego.
Leave it at the door.

The ego is difficult to tame.
But it's exhausting. It's financially draining.
And you end up playing someone else's game.

Acknowledge the ego. Face it. Then, rise above it.

Stay true to yourself. Stay authentic. Every single time.

Mistake #7: Not Understanding the Dark Side of Compounding

Compound interest is a double-edged sword.
It can be your best friend. Or your worst enemy.
Just depends on which side you're playing on.

Compounding is great for investments.
A nightmare for debt.

For those with high-interest debt, compounding turns into the evil villain.
Paying interest on interest.
The reason it feels like the outstanding amount on a credit card just never seems to go down.

Taking a loan can be a good thing.
To help build assets, like your education.
To help you save money.
To help refinance high-interest loans.

Taking loans at high interest rates can be a terrible thing.

When you buy things to flash the 'I've made it!'
sign.
When you use it to make investments that don't
outpace the interest you pay.
When you don't have the means to pay it off.

**Financially smart people take loans, even if
they can afford it, to save money.**
**Financially weak people take loans, knowing
that they can't afford them, to spend money!**

Mistake #8: Not Understanding That Most Purchases Have a Hidden Cost

I took a loan to invest in real estate.
Assuming that the price appreciation would take care of the interest rate I paid.

I forgot the hidden fees—registration, the brokerage, the capital gains tax on selling.
Taxes and Inflation. Yup, missed those too.
All of which reduced the actual return I made.

This isn't just about property.
Most things come with hidden costs.
Flight tickets. Gadgets. Cars. Investments.
Sneaky processing fees. Charges if you change your mind.
Subscriptions that auto-renew when you least expect.
The so-called 'convenience' fees. Yeah, pretty inconvenient, actually!

Some fees are negligible. Others are not.

Before you buy, do your research. Read the fine print.
You can't avoid every hidden cost, but at least you know what you're signing up for.

Mistake #9: Relying on One Job to Build Your Wealth

One income stream. One salary.

All eggs in one basket—we know how that story ends.

Job requirements evolve. Industries shift.

Your employer determines your value and your salary.

One shake-up and you're off track.

In a world where change is the only constant, broaden your horizon.

Keep your day job but build income streams beyond it.

- Invest
- Start a business or a side gig
- Create intellectual property
- Consult or coach
- Teach
- Freelance
- Build a personal brand

Your salary is not enough.
Diversify your income. Just like your investments.

My poor dad said, 'I can't afford it.'
My rich dad asked, 'How can I afford it?'
The first one lets you off the hook.
The second one forces you to think.

—Adapted from Robert Kiyosaki's
Rich Dad Poor Dad

Mistake #10: Not Creating a Margin of Safety

Hope is great.

Blind optimism is not.

The most important thing is to plan for this one question:

What if things don't work out as you think they will?

Always have a buffer.

Build that emergency fund.

Get health insurance.

Get life insurance, especially if your family leans on you financially.

Hope for the best.

Prepare for the unexpected.

Mistake #11: Believing That Someone Can Get Wealthy, Only by Taking from Someone Else

Growing up, I hated money.

We didn't have it, so I thought it was the cause of all our problems.

I hated rich people as well. (Because, why do things in half measures? Hate everything and everyone!)

I thought they were shrewd and corrupt.

I believed that someone got rich only by driving someone else to poverty.

Wealth was a zero-sum game to me.

Today I realize that my ignorance about wealth drove my emotions.

Everybody can create value.

Everybody can build wealth.

It doesn't have to come at anybody's expense.

There can be multiple winners.

In the game of money. In the game of life.

Mistake #12: Believing That Investing Is a Quick Race to Riches

Investing is not speculation.
Investing is not making money to impress someone.
If done right, investing your money can be one of the most fulfilling things you do.
If done right, investing is a long-term game to build wealth.

The fastest way to become wealthy is to go slow.
The earlier you start, the better.
The longer your money is invested, the better.

Growing up, I saw queues for everything, from milk to phone connections.
We had no choice but to be patient.
And so, we learnt patience.
You might not know that world.
But teach yourself patience.
Because life's best rewards take time.

Mistake #13: Not Realizing That the System Is Designed to Keep You Poor

We've been trying to play the system our whole lives.

In reality, the system has been playing us.

The system wants you to take loans at high interest rates.

It wants you to keep spending on credit cards.

It wants you to desire things and buy them on EMIs.

It sells desires. It sells aspirations.

Even if you do not have the capacity to afford them.

It sells ideas of success.

Even if those ideas are not your own.

Pay later. Pay the bare minimum.

That's how it earns.

The system wants you to burn your money in an FD.

It offers you interest rates equal to or lower than inflation under the garb of safety.
Money that they can then loan you back at higher interest.

The system encourages you to have one job.
To be dependent on that one income stream.
So that you take loans.
So that you can never leave your job.

The system endorses the consumerist society.
Buy, flaunt, repeat.
This is trending, it tells you.
Implying, shouldn't you get one too?
844 people bought this, it tells you.
Implying, can't you afford one too?

The system wants you to make impulse buys.
The 15% discount will end in 3.22 minutes.
It tells you it's super convenient.
1-click buy and you're done.

The system draws battle lines.
Between you and your friends. You and your
peers. You and the world.
The system makes us want what the
other has.

'If you only wished to be happy, this
could be easily accomplished;
but we wish to be happier than other
people; and this is always difficult;
for we believe others to be happier than
they are.'

—Montesquieu

Think about This

Perfection isn't the starting line—action is!
You don't need to have perfect knowledge, perfect data or the perfect income to start your money management journey.
You don't need to be perfect, either!

Make your own mistakes.
Learn from the mistakes of others.
Refine. Rework. It will be a continuous process.

Start.
Because starting imperfectly is way, way better than not starting at all.

Do This

- Pause, reflect!
  Note down:

  What are the mistakes you've been making with money?

  _____

  What could you have done differently? How?

  _____

  How can you do it differently, going forward?

  _____

AS LONG AS I
KNOW THIS

'Don't believe everything that you feel.
Not every feeling is a fact.
Don't believe everything that you think.
Not every thought is the truth.'

—Unknown

I believed that building wealth was about numbers.
The amount we earn. Then save. Then invest. Then get as returns.
I believed that I was a rational money manager.
Who made data-driven objective decisions.

Yet, when faced with real-world choices:
- Buy a house or rent?
- Take a loan now or wait?
- Start-up or a job?
- Pick stocks or mutual funds?

I realized:
Numbers don't drive money decisions.
Our biases do.
Our emotions do.
And our emotions make us do some very stupid things.

Today, I know that we are all prone to biases that we don't even know we have.

Sellers capitalize on this, so no choice is ever presented in a neutral manner.
No one is immune.

'Money has a little to do with how smart you are and a lot to do with how you behave. And behaviour is hard to teach, even to really smart people.'

—Morgan Housel

We're drowning in information. And jargon.
Not to mention, well-meaning relatives, who keep telling us how much we should have been earning and how Sharmaji *ka beta* owns a BMW at the age of 26!

How can one human being take it all in? We can't.
So our brain hits the easy button. Auto mode.

But here's the thing.
That auto mode is not driven by logic.

It's driven by our past experiences, our perception of the world and our emotions.

And by years of conditioning of the human mind!

When it comes to money, these biases make us act in irrational (aka crazy) ways.

If you're aware of these biases, you're halfway to winning already.

Skim through this chapter.

If you find yourself saying, 'OMG—that is so me,' you know what you've got to be watching out for!

Bias #1: Anchoring Bias

Relying too heavily on the first piece of information you receive.

Say you're shopping for a phone.
The first one you like is for ₹75,000.
No way! Way over your budget.
The next one you like is for ₹45,000.
Oh, that sounds like a great deal. You buy it!

EVEN though it was above your budget.
Because anything below your first reference point—₹75,000—seems like a good deal.
The first 75,000 anchored you.

If you don't have your own anchor, you borrow someone else's.

Now, say you're buying an apartment.
You're not too sure about prices in the area.
Along comes the agent: *'Another flat here just went for ₹70 lakh.'*

Boom! The anchor has been dropped.
You will now end up buying something around
₹70 lakh.

Anchoring bias is like having a financial GPS that's stuck on the wrong destination. You'll keep following its directions, even when you've long since missed the turn.

Bias #2: Availability Bias

Easily recalled, easily available information gets the VIP treatment from us.

Our brains love the freshest, most accessible info.
No matter where it comes from.

We hear of a colleague who got rich investing in a specific company.
We want to jump in.

We see headlines on a major stock-market dip.
It's trending everywhere.
We're ready to panic-sell. Even if long-term trends suggest stability.

We hear of a hot new crypto on social media.
People posting that they've made lakhs in 3 days.
We want to know how to buy in ASAP.

We decide based on what is easily available.
We decide based on what we remember most.
The buzz from cafés, social media and viral news—those become our financial compass.
We don't question the reliability of the information.

We prefer wrong information to no information.
Anything silent or invisible we downgrade.
It doesn't need to be the truest thing, as long as it's the loudest.

Fight availability bias.
Choose logic over hype. Choose facts over fiction.
Every single time.

Availability bias is like a Netflix recommendation algorithm for your brain. It keeps suggesting the same old shows (thoughts) because they're easy to recall, even if there are better options out there.

Bias #3: Loss Aversion Bias

We care more about avoiding losing ₹1000 than we care about winning ₹1000.

Sounds strange, but that's how our brains work. We're wired to feel the pain of a loss way more than the happiness from a gain of the same size.

This bias makes our money decisions a bit, well, bonkers.
It makes us want to avoid losses at all costs.
We'd rather not lose than gain.
We'd rather settle for the comfort of low or no returns (FDs, anyone?) than take smart risks that could help us meet our goals.

We hold on to investments that haven't done well for 5 years.
Because that would mean making the loss real.
Or we bought an asset and it drops in value—we panic and sell.
Only to regret when it rises again.

Pro tip: Sold an asset? Don't keep checking on it. Let it go.

If you keep obsessing over losses, you can't enjoy your wins.

+Pro tip: Bought an asset? Don't keep checking on it.

Let it bake.

It doesn't perform any better if you keep checking on it every day.

Loss aversion bias: the reason we sit through a terrible movie until the end than admit we made a poor investment.

Bias #4: Herding

The following-the-crowd bias.

Remember, as kids, we always felt that the best places to eat at or shop at were the ones with the longest lines?

We like fitting in. Being part of the cool crowd.
We like knowing that we're doing what everyone else is doing.
Even if no one else knows what they're doing.

Sometimes it works well.
You want to try a new restaurant.
5000 reviews, 4.8-star rating.
Let's do it!

Sometimes it doesn't work too well.
Word spreads that a particular city is the next big thing. THE place to be.
Suddenly, everyone's buying property there.
Inflating prices. Bubble!

Sometimes it doesn't work well at all.

Rumours that a bank is facing liquidity issues.

Customers rush to withdraw their money, fearing they'll lose it.

The bank is fundamentally sound, but it doesn't matter any more.

The herd-run has completely jeopardized its stability.

It's great for the smaller decisions—cafés, dinner choices, weekend spots.

For major financial decisions herding isn't the best way to go.

Consider all sides, then figure out your shit for yourself.

Investing with the herd is like following a GPS blindly—you might end up being stuck in traffic, but at least you're not stuck alone!

Bias #5: The Ostrich Effect

If it's negative information, you don't know and you don't want to know.

Say you've been spending a lot lately. More than you should.
Swiping that card. Racking up some debt.
You know you should check your bank balance, but you don't.
You know you should check how much you owe, but you'd rather not find out.

It's making you super anxious.
So, you shove that thought to the back of your mind. Continue swiping.
Cross your fingers, hoping it'll all go away.

Classic ostrich move, burying our heads in the sand and hoping for the best.

Ignoring problems doesn't make them vanish.
But we still think: 'If I can't see it, it doesn't exist.'

The ostrich effect: Because burying your financial problems in imaginary sand is easier than facing your bank statements!

Bias #6: Decision Fatigue

We make worse decisions at the end of the day.
We make worse decisions when we're tired.

Apparently, an average adult makes about 35,000 decisions a day.
Yep, that's a lot.
As decisions pile up, the quality drops.
The brain wants shortcuts when it's tired.
We enter the 'who cares' territory, where all decisions are made on impulse.
Hello, decision fatigue!

We spend (at least) 8 hours a day working for money.
Best not to let decision fatigue attack the same money.

The best thing is to reduce money decisions wherever you can.

– Automate
Automate bills, investments and savings. To go out directly from your account.

Fewer money decisions, less stress.
Then, apply automation to your life—what else can you run on auto?

- Keep things simple
Minimize the number of bank accounts you have.
Minimize the number of cards you have.
Less tracking, less juggling.

- Avoid big money decisions when you're hungry. Or lonely. Or tired.
Nothing more to add here. You know what to do.

Decision fatigue is the reason why, by the time you get to the end of the buffet, you end up with a plate full of everything, because choosing between everything felt like a high-stakes investment decision!

Bias #7: Sunk Cost Fallacy

We've already started, so we may as well keep going!
Even if things aren't working for us any more.

We stick with a plan because we've already invested time, effort or money into it.
Even when it's clear we're chasing a lost cause.

Say you've been working on a start-up idea. It's not getting anywhere.
But you continue pouring money into the idea because, 'I have spent years working on it.'
You have to make it worth it!

No, you don't.
Not if it stopped making sense a long time back.

Same with money.
Sometimes investments don't pan out.
We continue with them, anyway.
We can't lose a rupee of what we've invested!

Yes, you can.

If it's not working, it's not.
If it's gone, it's gone.
Look at your choices as separate events instead of one big scenario.
Don't throw good money after bad money.

Rather than doubling down, admit a bad choice and move forward.
Onwards and upwards!

The sunk cost fallacy: Where yesterday's losses become today's excuses for tomorrow's bad decisions.

Bias #8: Gambler's Fallacy

Past events will influence future events.
Even if these events have nothing to do with each other!

You tossed a coin 9 times and, shockingly, all 9 times you got a heads.
Let me ask you: What is the likely outcome of the 10th toss?
Chances are high that you will say tails.
Because the universe owes us a tails after a string of heads.

Sorry, brain, that's not how probability rolls.
There is no 'correction' process due.
Every coin toss is independent of the last. No hidden memory. No vendetta. Only chance.

Our brain makes us only notice the times when 2 things, coincidentally, appear next to each other.
And we ignore all the times they don't.

So we jump into a stock just because it hit its an annual low. It has to climb now!

No, it doesn't.

Or we sell fantastic stocks fearing that their winning streak is too long. They have to come down now.

No, they don't.

Each event is a beginning.

Not a continuation of previous events.

Lead with logic.

Believing in the gambler's fallacy is like expecting Domino's to bring you a pizza with a different topping this time because you've had the same one 3 times in a row. Sometimes, you just get what you ordered!

Bias #9: Framing Effect

No information is presented in a neutral manner.
Given 2 options, we'll always pick a story we like.

Our choices are based on presentation, not content.
Sellers are on to this.

Consider this: '70% fat-free' vs '30% fat'.
Same thing, different presentation.
The way it's spun makes all the difference.

Here's a trick question.
Here are 2 investment options for you. Which one is better?
- A well-diversified portfolio that has a 70% chance of gains.
- A well-diversified portfolio that has a 30% chance of losing money.

Okay, it wasn't tricky.
It's the same thing, framed differently.
But the first message we like. The second, not so much.

Here's another for you to pick from:

- A mutual fund that has beaten the market benchmark by 5% over the last year.
- A mutual fund that has beaten the benchmark by 2% each year over the last 3 years.

Most investors would probably pick the first.

It shows the highest rate of return over the immediate past year.

But in reality, both tell us nothing about the future.

Everyone loves a good spin. But watch for the framing!

It's the facts that count. Not just the pretty parts.

The framing effect is like putting a fancy frame around a potato and calling it art. Don't let a pretty picture make you forget you're still dealing with a potato.

Bias #10: Mental Accounting

Our brains label money. Like filing stuff in folders.
Each label changes how we feel and use that money.

Mental accounting is our brain's slightly weird cashier.
It helps us keep track of what we spend.
Gives us a ballpark for a 'fair' price.
Allows us to make quick decisions.

But, sometimes, it's too creative.
It tells us that all money is not equal.

It depends on how we earned it.

You find ₹500 on the road.
Party money! 'Let's go, guys, dinner's on me!'
But what about that phone you've been saving for?
Nah, this isn't phone money.

This is 'lucky, treat-yourself' money.

Same with birthday cash, tax refunds, sudden windfalls.
Surprise money just feels different.
Easy come, easy go.

It depends on how we use it.

₹150 every day on a cup of coffee and 2 samosas? Cool.
But, a one-time ₹5000 buy? 'Whoa, let's slow down. Can't afford that!'

It depends on how it makes us feel. <3

Paying ₹5000 in a restaurant in your city vs paying ₹5000 in a restaurant in Goa.
In your own city, you're outraged. 'Bro, are they kidding?'
In Goa, it's all about the feels.
Our logic takes a holiday, along with us.

Same with buying a drink in a movie theatre, at a cricket match or a concert.

We're willing to pay twice as much.

After all, the supermarket doesn't give you the same experience.

We think that circumstances are different.
Unfortunately, the impact on our bank accounts is the same.

Companies are on to this.

- Credit cards—like a magic wallet of never-ending money!
- Luxury buys—we're premium, the price is premium.
- Special days—of course, flowers will be more expensive on Valentine's Day. All part of the special-day experience. Do it for the sake of love!

This is why budgeting isn't just for nerds.

It helps you set boundaries—spending, saving, investing.

Within those boundaries, you have total freedom!
Stay sorted, stay smart!

Mental accounting is when you treat your money like a box of chocolates, assigning different financial flavours to each rupee.

Bias #11: The Dunning–Kruger Effect

The less you know, the more you think you know.

The more you know, the easier you think it is for everyone else.

Watching 3 reels on personal finance (or even making them) does not make us experts.

If we think we know everything about money, we most likely do not.

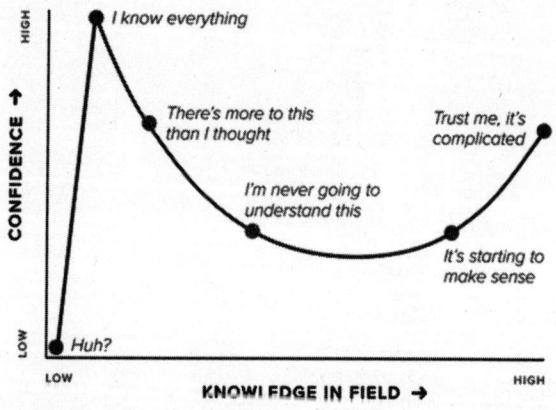

It's never the experts who say, 'I know everything.' It's always the uninformed who are the most confident.

Keep digging deeper, keep learning.
A little knowledge can be a dangerous thing!

The Dunning–Kruger effect is proof that some people don't just believe they're the smartest in the room; they believe they're the smartest in every room, even if it's an empty one.

Bias #12: Social Comparison Bias

You determine your own value based on how you stack up against others.

We can't help checking out what others are doing.
Your friend's investing in crypto. She's got a new car.
Suddenly, your mutual fund seems like crap.
Your bike doesn't feel as cool.

It's financial FOMO.
We're always peeking over the fence, thinking our neighbour's grass is greener.

Financial advisers love and hate this.
It helps them sell products—love.
It also means they spend time convincing clients not to follow the herd—hate.

Remember: Your money. Your choices.
Be you, not someone else.
You're amazing, anyway!

Social comparison bias is the financial equivalent of trying to fit into a pair of tight jeans just because your neighbour wears them.

Bias #13: The 'I'm-Not-Biased' Bias

I thought of ALL my friends reading about biases.
Me? Oh, no. No biases here!

Biases are our brain's built-in default settings.
They drive our decisions on autopilot.
Based on what our family tells us.
Based on what the media shows us.
Based on what society expects from us.

We think we're not biased, but no one is completely self-aware. No one!

We all highlight the best bits about ourselves.
Job interviews, dates—we're all about selling the 'perfect' us.

Come to terms with the idea that we are all prone to cognitive biases.
They can make us our own worst enemies.
No matter how smart we are.

When you realize you are as biased as everyone else, you've won.
Stay aware.
Protect that money. From, well, yourself. ;)

The 'I'm-not-biased' bias is like saying you're the world's best chef while burning Maggi.

'My favourite bias is the "I'm not biased" bias . . . The brighter you are, the harder it can be to see your own limitations. Being good at thinking can make you worse at rethinking.'

—Adam Grant

Do This

- Pause, reflect!
  Note down:

  In what ways am I biased?

  _____

  How do these biases affect my financial decisions?

  _____

  How do these biases affect my life?

  _____

Do I want to overcome these biases?
  - If not, why? What's stopping me?

  _____

  - If yes, what steps can I take?

  _____

OH! ONE LAST THING

I hope that one day you look at yourself and find everything you ever wanted.

May 2003

At the age of 50, my parents decided to buy a house.

After 2 decades of moving from one rented house to another.

They were tired. Physically. Emotionally.

The house, in a faraway suburb of Delhi, named Faridabad, would cost ₹10 lakh.

It wasn't a small amount at the time. Not for them.

A loan of ₹8 lakh was somehow arranged.

No bank would give them a loan.

So, they took one from a non-banking financial corporation (NBFC).

At an exorbitant rate of interest.

They finally bought the house.

I was in the US.

Doing a PhD in physics.

100% scholarship—because that was the only way we could have afforded that education.

Dad had taken a loan of ₹55,000 for my one-way ticket.

As a student, I was paid a generous stipend every month: $1350!

That was a lot of money.

The kind of money I had never seen in my life.

For 2 years, I lived like a miser.

Cooked my own food, washed my own clothes, did not go out, did not travel, walked as much as I could, bought stuff from the supermarket.

Saved as much as I could.

Things were starting to look up—parents had a new house. I had my $$$ savings!

August 2004

Dad was let go from his job.

He couldn't get another one.
So he decided to start out on his own.
Unfortunately, that didn't work out.

There was no money coming in.
Our expenses didn't stop—households, utilities, my sister's education.
Plus, the home loan EMIs.

In 1 year, everything changed. Our world had turned upside down.

Dad called me, checking if I had money to spare.
'Yes, Papa. I have money right now.'
'Thank you. Thank you so much.'
As he said this, he broke down.

He was embarrassed. That he had to ask his young son for money.
He was relieved that I had money to spare.
He was tired. That nothing seemed to work out, no matter how much he tried.
He was hopeless. Wondering if things were ever going to go right.

At that moment, I HATED MONEY.
Hated what it had done to us in all these years.
Hated what it was doing to us.

I told myself that I would never let money have
so much power over me.
I told myself that I would do things differently.

I never ever wanted to be in a position where
money could rule over me.

But I made a mistake because of this attitude.
I disrespected money.
I thought since I could always make it, I didn't
need to protect it.
I didn't need to grow it.
I was wrong.

March 2019
At 39, history repeated for me.
I had stepped down as the CEO of my start-up
6 months earlier.
Was still figuring out what to do in life.

Had no savings, because all my money had been invested in my start-up.

I was unemployed. With no money and no source of income.
I'd reached the exact same point as my father.

I started to give corporate talks, to earn money, while I tried to figure out what to do next.

And then Covid happened.
The entire world stopped.
So did my only income stream.

I had 5 months' worth of money left in the bank—to pay for the home EMI, school fees, living expenses.
I had to start all over again.

All these years, I'd thought I was doing things differently, by earning well, by showing money the middle finger.
I wasn't.

Different Journeys. Same Destination.

We're told that money is a private matter.
We talk about everything else—the weather, the news, the neighbours.
But. We. Never. Talk. About. Money.

What we earn, how we invest, the loans we take—these topics are off limits.
Almost taboo.
Parents will ask when we're starting a family, but never when we're starting our SIP.

So we end up making mistakes.
Our own mistakes.

I don't regret the mistakes I've made.
They've shaped me, made me who I am today.
But my beliefs about money held me back.
They clouded my vision, made me misjudge people, situations, the world.
They were misconceptions that I lived with for a large part of my life.

You don't have to.

To my 20-year-old self this is what I'd say.
What I wish I'd known.

To everyone like me—this is what I'd like to tell you.
What I'd like to leave you with.

Letters I Would Write to the 20-Year-Old Ankur

#1
dear ankur,
You have a 'relationship' with money.
Everyone does. Even if you think you don't.

You have that one story that's shaped how you will interact with money.
Even if you don't know what it is.

Think about it—that one big event growing up.
Or a series of small events that add up. It's important.

What you believe about money will influence everything. Without your even knowing it.
It will drive your career choices.
It will have a say in your relationships.
It will dictate your emotions. Your worries.
It will impact your health.

Your relationship with money will shape your relationship with life.

love,

#2
dear ankur,
Since you grew up without much money, either of these 3 things will happen:
- You'll spend your entire life chasing money, or
- You'll spend your entire life trying to escape money, or
- You'll spend your entire life going beyond money.

Those who chase money, see money as a powerful, unattainable thing.
Those who escape money, see money as a scary thing.
Those who go beyond money, see money as a beautiful thing.

You may not know it today, but the choice—deciding which way to go—is yours.
Choose wisely.

love,

#3
dear ankur,
The chase for money can be an endless one.
The constant running and the stress.
The pride in the things you have.
The anxiety about the things you don't have.
The desire for just one more thing.

You'll start believing that money is your end goal.

Don't forget that the only thing you actually wanted was happiness—that's the reason you were chasing money in the first place!

love,

#4
dear ankur,
Money will not change you.
It will reveal you.

If you are an inherently kind person, money will make you kinder.
If you are an inherently charitable person, money will make you more charitable.
If you are an inherently proud person, money will make you prouder.

If you're a worrier today, you'll be a worrier tomorrow,
Today, you'll worry about being able to afford vegetables. Tomorrow you'll worry about being able to afford cars.
The amount of stress will remain the same.

Money will escalate your strengths.
Money will intensify your flaws.
It will just make you more of who you already are.

love,

#5
dear ankur,
Earning money is not the same as keeping money.
Being rich is not the same as being wealthy.

Earning money doesn't mean you'll save.
Saving money doesn't mean you'll invest.
Investing money doesn't mean you'll invest wisely.
Keeping money is far, far more difficult than making money.

Look around you.
Skilled, hard-working people. Earning money.
Struggling to keep it.

Stuck with debt and loans that are difficult to pay off.

Think of the athletes, musicians and celebrities who go from being super rich to filing for bankruptcy.
They've earned more money than anyone can dream of.
They just didn't know how to keep it.

The difference between a rich and a wealthy person is how sustainable that wealth is.
Being rich = things people have that we can see.
True wealth = things people have that we can't see!

love,

#6
dear ankur,
Don't hate money—it's important.
It buys you peace of mind. It buys you health. It buys you safety. It buys you comfort.

Above all, money will give you courage.
To start a new business.
To quit a bad job. To quit a bad boss.
To take a gap year to follow your passion.
To walk out of a bad relationship.
To move across cities. Across countries.
To believe in yourself.

A lot of things we think require courage actually just require money.

love,

#7
dear ankur,
It's okay . . .
To wear old clothes.
To not upgrade your phone.
To buy second-hand items.
To live in a simple house.

No one expects you to be rich in your 20s.
Don't pretend to be.

People may expect you to be rich in your 30s.
Doesn't matter. Don't pretend to be.

People's attention is short-lived.
They move on, and we wait for another chance
to impress.
It's a never-ending cycle.

**In a status-driven rat race you can never win.
There'll always be someone who has bigger,
shinier and more expensive things than you.
Spare yourself this.**

Just know that no one's thinking about you, as
much as you are.
Just like you, they're all too busy thinking about
themselves!
It's okay to live a simple life.
It's okay to live below your means.

Use that extra cash to give yourself the best gift.
A life where you don't have to worry about money.

love,

#8

dear ankur,

Money is never more important than your relationships.

Money is never more important than love.

Work and money will make you think that your relationships can wait.

It will tell you that the call to your parents can wait.

That saying 'I love you' to your family can wait.

That spending time with them can wait.

Money will tempt you into thinking, 'This is the time to build a career. Make money. Everything else can be postponed. Family and relationships can wait.'

Don't fall for it.

Money matters. But relationships matter more.

If you die, your company will put up a job posting in 48 hours.

As much as money and your job are important, do not ignore relationships.
Especially the ones in which you remain irreplaceable.

love,

#9
dear ankur,
Having less doesn't make you poor.
Always wanting more does.

A person who makes ₹3 lakh per year but only needs ₹2 lakh to be happy is wealthier than the person who makes ₹10 lakh but needs ₹20 lakh to be happy.
Read that again.

love,

#10

dear ankur,

Today you think that you're not wealthy because your parents keep making poor decisions.

When you look back at your life, you'll realize that it isn't always your parents' fault.

The decisions they take may not always work out.
Doesn't mean the decisions they take are wrong.

No one knows before taking a decision whether or not it will work out.
We only know once we have taken it.

Keep this in mind when you're judging others.
Keep this in mind when you're judging yourself.

Don't be too impressed with yourself.
You may not be as good as you think you are.
Don't be too hard on yourself.
You're never as bad as you think you are.

love,

#11

dear ankur,
Building wealth—and everything worth building—requires time. Effort. Commitment.

Saving is hard.
Being broke is harder.

Learning about investments is hard.
Suffering from bad investments is harder.

Paying off debt is hard.
Letting your debt compound is harder.

Choose your hard.

love,

#12

dear ankur,
No matter how hard the times are, how stuck you feel, how difficult it is, remember, you'll figure a way out.

Today, all you know is that there isn't enough money.
Today, all you can think about is how Ma has to keep hunting around the house for hidden or forgotten currency notes.
Just to make ends meet.

She looks in every corner possible.
She finds a ₹10 note. A ₹50 note. A ₹20 note.
Hidden somewhere yesterday, discovered today.
Enough to manage today.
Until another day requires her to do the same.

Twenty years from now, you'll realize it's a life lesson.
No matter how hard things seem, there are always corners that will get you out.
Just keep looking for those corners.

love,

#13

dear ankur,

You're struggling with money—you're not alone.
You're struggling with life—you're not alone.

Everyone is confused. Even if they don't tell you that they are.
Everyone is unsure. Even if they don't show you that they are.
Everyone is figuring it out.

Whenever you're in doubt, bet on the only thing you can bet on.
Yourself.
Life will show you a way.
It'll all be okay.
You will be okay.
Hugs!

'I'm still learning to love the parts of myself that no one claps for.'

—Rudy Francisco

Think about This

What are the 5 things you are going
to take away from this book?

_____

_____

_____

_____

_____

You're ready to start, my friend.
Be optimistic. Be confident.
Feel good about yourself.
You've got this!

DISCLAIMER

I am not one to post disclaimers. But since this is a book involving money, I feel the need to.

3 critical disclaimers:

1. I am not a finance expert. I am not SEBI certified. I do not have a finance degree. I have no business writing a book on money. So please, do not take anything I say in this book at face value.

    I trust you with your intelligence and judgement, and believe you will do your homework before following anything that I say in this book.

2. I have mentioned a lot of brands in this book. None of them are aware of it, and none of them have paid me to do so.

I have worked (and still work) with some of them, commercially. But those are one-time campaigns and do not extend to this book. Disclosure:

I am not an investor in any of the companies that I have mentioned in the book.

3. Whatever I share in this book is through the lens of my own life.

    Which, I recognize and fully respect, may not work for you.

    It is called personal finance for a reason—it is personal.

    The objective of the book is not to tell you what to do. It is to show you what can be done.

    Ultimately, the path will be specific to you, unique to you, chosen by you.

That's all for the disclaimers.

No lawyers were harmed, used or consulted in writing the above.
Straight from the heart.

ACKNOWLEDGEMENTS

This book has written itself over a span of 30 years.

Through the experiences I have had with money, the mistakes I have made with it, the content I have been creating over the past 18 years, the videos that people have so lovingly received over the past 3.5 years, and the thousands of comments that told me how I could do better.

What you hold in your hand, though, would not have been possible if it weren't for Elaine and Anabelle, who painstakingly went through all of that content, weaved it into words that you have consumed and edited it innumerable times so as to make it as easy to comprehend as possible.

Thank you, Bubbs and Belle—I am so glad we went for dinner that day :)

Big thanks to the entire Penguin Random House India team for never making me feel, even for a second, that I was doing it all by myself. You made this book as much yours as I made it mine.

Thanks to Bali and Singla for teaching me about money in your own ways. I don't think you realize how much that shaped me up foundationally.

Thanks to Ruchi, whose money approach gave me the courage to fight the mistakes I made and recover from them. I am so glad we went through all that we did.

But the biggest thanks is reserved for you— the one holding the book. Your love, feedback, appreciation and criticism defined me and continue to do so. Every single day I pinch myself in disbelief that I get to live a life where millions of people tell me what I am doing well and where I can improve.

Thank you, forever.

This is ankur warikoo, signing off :)

ABOUT THE AUTHOR

Ankur Warikoo is an entrepreneur based in India and is one of India's top content creators. He currently runs WebVeda, an online school for young professionals. Ankur is an angel investor, and in his spare time he loves to mentor entrepreneurs.

He is also a bestselling author. His first book, *Do Epic Shit*, was published in December 2021 and hit the #1 bestseller spot. His second book, *Get Epic Shit Done*, was published in December 2022 and hit the #1 spot again.

Previously, Ankur founded nearbuy.com and was its CEO, from its inception in 2015 until 2019. Prior to that, he was the founding CEO of Groupon India (2011–15) and head of Groupon APAC (2013–15).

Ankur holds an MBA degree from the Indian School of Business. He also has an MS degree in physics from Michigan State University and a BS degree in physics from Hindu College, Delhi University.

Ankur was part of *Fortune* magazine's '40 under 40' list for India; *Forbes* magazine's 'Top 100 Digital Creators' list for 2022; LinkedIn India's 'Top Voices' for 2018, 2019 and 2020; LinkedIn India's 'Spotlight' list; and *Business Today*'s 'India's Top Executives under 40' list.

He stays in Delhi with his wife and 2 kids.

Scan QR code to access the
Penguin Random House India website